D0428667

MAKING A
DIFFERENCE

{
dif·fer·ence

[dif-er-uhns, dif-ruhns]

verb - a significant change in

or effect on a situation
}

MAKING A DIFFERENCE

A MATTER OF PURPOSE, PASSION & PRIDE

STEVE GILLILAND

Published by Advantage, Charleston, South Carolina.
Member of Advantage Media Group.

ADVANTAGE is a registered trademark and the Advantage colophon is a trademark of Advantage Media Group, Inc.

Printed in the United States of America.

ISBN: 978-1-59932-260-5
LCCN: 2011903883

This publication is designed to provide accurate and authoritative information in regard to the subject matter covered. It is sold with the understanding that the publisher is not engaged in rendering legal, accounting, or other professional services. If legal advice or other expert assistance is required, the services of a competent professional person should be sought.

Advantage Media Group is proud to be a part of the Tree Neutral® program. Tree Neutral offsets the number of trees consumed in the production and printing of this book by taking proactive steps such as planting trees in direct proportion to the number of trees used to print books. To learn more about Tree Neutral, please visit www.treeneutral.com. To learn more about Advantage's commitment to being a responsible steward of the environment, please visit www.advantagefamily.com/green

Advantage Media Group is a leading publisher of business, motivation, and self-help authors. Do you have a manuscript or book idea that you would like to have considered for publication? Please visit www.amgbook.com or call 1.866.775.1696

CONTACT STEVE

To schedule Steve to speak at your event, call:

866-445-5452

For more information, go to

www.stevegilliland.com

Dedicated
to the most important person
in my life,

my wife, Diane.

Meeting her shaped my heart
and changed my life.

ACKNOWLEDGMENTS

I have been blessed with an especially large and dedicated group of people who have supported, encouraged, inspired and challenged me to make a difference. The connection I have made with people from all walks of life has been a great source of energy and satisfaction for me.

My sons Stephen and Josh and stepsons, Adam and Alex, mean everything to me. My greatest joy is spending time with them and their families. My daughters-in-law Amanda and Kari are wonderful and my grandson, Karter Paul, keeps me young.

My companion and confidant, Diane, has brought me contentment which is something I wasn't sure I would experience in this lifetime. In addition, I am grateful to my staff who support me every day. They juggle the constant flood of information and requests that come through my office, and are always looking for new opportunities to grow our business.

I am also grateful to my friends Skip and Sharon Alberts, Mike and Cheryl Cassel, Lance and Lynn Crumley, Jeff and Laurie Dray, Scott and Melanie Epperson, Tony and Amy Holcomb, Bruce and Fran Montgomery and Jason and Brandy Rosenberger. A special thank you to my friend Todd Crissman, who has been alongside me for the past 23 years.

A unique expression of gratefulness is due to my former secretary, Margaret Shannon, who blessed me with her extraordinary wisdom and knowledge. This book is a further tribute to her astuteness and acumen. Margaret supplied me with volumes of inspiring scripts she had attained throughout the years. She may well have written this book.

I am beholden to the various authors and speakers who have influenced my writing over the better part of three decades. The numerous books I have read and a number of seminars I attended have assisted my personal and professional development. As I have embarked on the writing of this book, omission of any appropriate acknowledgment is inadvertent and not deliberate.

To everyone who has been a part of my journey, thank you for making a difference and making it possible for me to give something back.

{
"Everybody can make a difference...
You don't have to make your subject
and verb agree to make a difference.
You only need a heart full of grace.
A soul generated by love."
}

Martin Luther King, Jr.

FOREWORD

This book demonstrates that you don't need a master's degree or a doctorate to make the world a better place. I have plenty of knowledge that didn't come from a formal education, just numerous experiences that taught me plenty. I became part of a revolution of inspired people who see the opportunity to change the world.

More than 38 years ago, Rollin King and I got together and decided to start a different kind of airline. We began with one simple notion: If you get your passengers to their destinations when they want to get there, on time, at the lowest possible fares and make darn sure they have a good time doing it, people will fly your airline. And you know what? We were right.

Since 1987 we have been *making a difference* in the airline industry. In view of that fact, The Department of Transportation began tracking customer satisfaction statistics in 1987, and Southwest has consistently led the entire airline industry with the lowest ratio of complaints per passengers boarded. Many airlines have tried to copy our business model, and the culture of Southwest is admired and emulated by corporations and organizations in all walks of life. We pioneered senior fares, a same-day air freight delivery service, and ticketless travel. We led the way with the first airline web page—southwest.com, DING! The first-ever direct link to customer's computer desktops that delivers live updates on the hottest deals, and the first airline corporate blog,

Nuts About Southwest. Our *Share the Spirit* community programs make Southwest the hometown airline of every city we serve.

As you read this book you will discover that making a difference is like innovation. People who make a difference have the capacity not just to envision something in an abstract, day-dreaming, fantasizing kind of way, but they have the capacity and drive to actually go out and do it. Steve Gilliland believes that the world has more good than bad and that each of us has the ability to make the good bigger, while shrinking the bad. His life's work is to serve others and influence them to do the same. He believes that no matter what you face each day, you have to remain determined to find a way to bring joy and hope to people around you. You have to focus on having calmness, compassion, humor and a positive attitude.

While we don't know what challenges face the people we meet every day, we do have the power to bring someone hope, if only for a moment. And as this book suggests, that hope can multiply a thousand times. This book also offers up a wonderful dose of how to make someone's day, but warns that in order to be inspiring you have to feel inspired. You have to fill your own cup first. If you are happy, then you will make other people happy. How you start your day will go a long way in determining the rest of it. This book is a positive look at what is necessary to make a difference and is a great reminder that Monday isn't designed to add depression to an otherwise happy week. Making a difference is about conscious choices that do, and will, impact the lives of people we encounter. It is about leaders in an organization who behave in such a manner that is congruent with the behavior they expect from their employees. It is about modeling the behavior you desire for the rest of the company. Your job gives you authority. Your behavior earns you respect.

This book is a simple yet profound idea that can change your life. You don't need money to make a difference, you just need to discover true wealth. Whenever you have someone else's attention, your actions can convince them that the world is a cold, frightening place, or that it's full of love and joy. I believe that once you have completed reading this book, you can inspire people everywhere to *make a difference*. One person can change the world. It starts with you!

Herb Kelleher
Co-founder, Chairman Emeritus and former CEO
Southwest Airlines

TABLE OF CONTENTS

PURPOSE...IT DRIVES YOU

PASSION...IT FUELS YOU

PRIDE...IT DEFINES YOU

INTRODUCTION: WHY ME?

Opening my eyes, I found myself waking up in a spacious king-size bed in an equally roomy three-room suite at the Gaylord Palms Hotel in Orlando, Florida. I was still grinning and almost laughing out loud at my astonishing reception from the evening before upon my arrival to the property. I had received some red carpet welcomes in my speaking career; however, this one would definitely top them all.

I arrived in Orlando, Florida on US Airways Flight 1709 at 6:17 PM. To the right of the escalator in the baggage claim area, I spotted a gentleman holding a sign with my last name on it. The client had pre-arranged a car service for me and the driver, David Cleator, only a few yards away, smiled at me and slowly raised the sign as if he had known me for years. I threaded my way through the dozens of people and when I got close enough David said, "Welcome to Orlando, Mr. Gilliland, how was your flight?" Taken aback because his demeanor was like seeing an old friend again, I inquired how he knew it was me. His explanation was even more astonishing. When he was hired to pick me up, he went on the internet and searched my name. He then proceeded to my website and watched my preview DVD and imprinted my face in his mind. WOW!

During the ride to the hotel, my attention was momentarily diverted from the soothing sound of the jazz CD David had inserted to overhearing his brief, but out of the ordinary, phone call. I heard him say, "We are about 10 minutes out. We should be arriving at 7:15 PM." Taking into account all of my previous experiences involving a car service, I couldn't recall any driver ever calling the hotel to announce our arrival. Then we arrived. My eyebrows rose. Three hotel employees awaited my arrival and before David could make his way to open my door, a youthful member of the bell staff beat him to it. "Mr. Gilliland, we have been expecting you!" With a stunned smile on my face, I exited the sedan and was enthusiastically introduced to three employees from the hotel, including the assistant general manager, front desk supervisor and Vinnie, an adolescent looking young man whose name badge also publicized his title beneath his name. Vinnie's title was "celebrity services."

Before entering the hotel, Mr. Cleator gave me the details of my return to the Orlando International Airport. As we strode into the grandiose lobby, Vinnie informed me that he already had my room key and would be escorting me to my room. He noticed my grateful smile and reciprocated with a boyish grin and asked, "More than you expected?" Most definitely! However, having stayed at two other Gaylord Entertainment properties in Nashville and Dallas, I was very familiar with the spacious design of their facilities. I made him aware of my thankfulness as we continued our passage toward my new home for this one evening. As we moved closer to an elevator, my inquisitiveness impelled me to ask a question which had been on my mind since I was first introduced to him. Just what did the position of celebrity services entail and why was he assigned to me? With a sheepish smirk he said, "I am one of six people assigned to escort all of the celebrities who stay at our property. It is my job responsibility to make sure you receive all the amenities deserving of someone who has achieved your level of success. From the moment you arrive until the minute you leave, our department has the enviable duty to make you feel welcome and special. Some of the other employees are always interrogating me about the conversations I have with our celebrity guests."

As we entered the elevator, Vinnie held the door opening to let me enter first. Endeavoring to hold back the laughter which was building up inside me, I asked, "Vinnie, exactly who am I?" "Sir, I am not sure I understand your question," he responded with the utmost esteem in his tone. Without hesitation I took him back to his explanation of what his position entailed and said, "If you are assigned to all the celebrities, then you must know who I am." Vinnie anxiously glanced away and then countered by saying, "Please don't be insulted, sir, but I don't have a 'freaking' clue." I laughed out loud and let him know his answer didn't insult me and was rather refreshing. "Well, then I am confused," he said with a puzzled look on his face. "The conference you are speaking at is one of the largest our hotel has ever hosted. In peeking at the conference program, I noticed it is attended by a variety of people from some extraordinarily prominent companies. And then add to the fact I have already escorted Michael Eisner from Walt Disney Company and Joe Theisman, the former quarterback of the Washington Redskins, who are both keynote speakers at this conference, like yourself. So my only question would be, again with no offense intended, why you?" Do the math, Vinnie. When you hire Michael Eisner, Joe Theisman and me to speak at the same conference, one thing is for certain. After the first two aforesaid agreed to speak at this conference, they discovered they were out of money and contacted me.

It seemed an eternity, but finally we arrived at my room, or shall I say luxury apartment. As we crossed the threshold of the entry way into the living room, Vinnie could see that I was more than impressed. He asked me what time I wanted a wakeup call and also what time I would like breakfast. Overwhelmed I said, "Breakfast!" He would explain to me that the breakfast of my choice would be delivered at whatever time I requested. He would personally place the order and guarantee the delivery within five minutes of my requested time. The next morning, at 6:00 AM, my favorite breakfast was served – eggs benedict. At 6:30 AM the phone rang and it was Vinnie. "Mr. Gilliland, what time would you like me to escort you to the staging area of the grand ballroom?" I let him know that 7:30 AM would be ideal and, just as you might expect, he was ringing my doorbell, yes doorbell, at 7:30 AM sharp.

As we proceeded down the hallway, he inquired about my night's sleep and also my breakfast. He then began telling me of the elaborate staging this association had designed for the conference. He explained that since he had been working at the hotel, he had never observed such an ostentatious set-up for a meeting. Four huge video monitors, a six-foot high stage and lighting that would rival the academy awards. The ballroom was set to seat 4,000 people and an overflow video monitor was constructed outside the room. Prior to arriving at the ballroom, he then said, "Can I ask you one more question?" I answered, "Sure." Moving to a standstill and facing me, he then asked his question. "How did you end up here? I mean, they didn't run out of money and you must be tremendously talented or they wouldn't have hired you. I went to your website last night and enjoyed getting to know you even better. But I just was curious – how did you end up where you are today?"

I paused for a breath, grinned and motioned Vinnie to come with me. Let me see how much time I can spare. We both sat down in two oversized chairs in the corridor of a long hallway and I unexpectedly took Vinnie back to the 90's. With his eyes affixed on me and his concentration on every word, I began my account of how I ended up in that exact moment being escorted by a gentleman who held the title of "celebrity services."

For many years, my greatest enemy was myself. Every mistake, every miscalculation, every stumble I made, I replayed in my mind again and again. Every broken promise just added to the enemy I was fighting living in my head. My dismay began to paralyze my thinking. I was failing miserably as a husband, father, brother and son. The woman I had promised everything felt like I had provided nothing, so she was satisfied to end our marriage. By the time I was 39 years old, I had no money, no hope and no purpose. As my sons grew older, I continued to doubt my beliefs and believe my doubts. My credit cards were maxed out and I was living contrary to everything I once believed was right. As I sat in a two-bedroom apartment on Christmas Eve, 1997 while my sons celebrated Christmas with their mom at her parents' house, tears began streaming down my face and all I could think about was that maybe someday my ex-wife could find a new husband and my sons would have a new father who wouldn't let them down.

"Why me?" were the only two words I kept repeating as I selfishly prayed and asked God to give me some course, or at least a calmness about my state of affairs. I cried myself to sleep that evening only to suddenly wake up to a dream that seemed as real as my circumstances. A person in the dream reiterated the phrase "why not you?" repeatedly. For days I couldn't stop thinking about the dream and the faceless person who was seemingly trying to bestow me advice. I endured the holidays and was back to my standard schedule. At the suggestion of a friend, I sought out a counselor to embark on a healing process that would prove to be a life-changing decision.

"Sit down," Herb Hayes said softly. Drawing a chair around to face me, he said, "Look here, Steve. When I begin to offer advice, it will be truth and may not be delivered with tact. I will tell you what you need to hear, not what you may want to hear. If I am going to help you, then you must do the same. You must be truthful with me and with yourself." Crossing his arms and leaning back in his chair he said, "You mentioned on the phone you had a dream that upset you. Why did it upset you?"

Because after praying that night and asking God "why me?", the faceless person in the dream kept saying again and again, "Why not you?" It troubles me because, for most of my life, I have been a good person who did what was right and thought I was an upright husband and father. I know I wasn't perfect, and I made a number of bad choices, but my present situation isn't of my making. I didn't choose to live in a two-bedroom apartment and be struggling financially. This wasn't my choice! "Steve, we are all in situations of our own choosing. Our thinking produces a course to success or failure. Years ago, you selected your path. You chose to get married when you were eighteen after your freshman year at college. You chose to transfer after your sophomore year and you chose to begin a family prior to your graduation. You chose to purchase a new car when you were 21 years old and you chose how many credit cards you would apply for. You chose to eat steak instead of hamburger and fast food instead of vegetables. You chose your household expenses! Years ago you began making choices that placed you in your present situation. When you say it wasn't your choice to live in a two-bedroom apartment and struggle financially, I must steadfastly disagree."

I may have contributed to my current situation, but she ultimately made the decision that put me here. I didn't want a divorce and even begged her not to leave. Herb looked at me and said, "It is your fault! She initiated the divorce because of the choices you made. She isn't without fault but you are here today because of your choices, not hers. Every unsuccessful person I know has never said it was their fault. You messed up and, by your own choosing, you are here. You are where you are because of your thinking. Your thinking dictates your decisions. Decisions are choices. The good news is that although you controlled your past and made bad choices, you now can control your future and make good decisions. Where you end up mentally, physically, spiritually, emotionally and financially will not be determined by anyone but you."

"Why me?" is a question that people have been asking themselves since time began. Steve, you are in the center of a self-absorbed pity party that rationalizes where you are and authorizes you to escape taking responsibility for your situation. I don't know who the man in your dream represents; however, I do know that he is right. You can spend the rest of your life blaming everything on everyone but yourself (why me), or you can take responsibility for your past and start a new chapter and embrace the challenges (why not me). Instead of reading the same page over and over, it is time for you to turn the page. It is time to start a new chapter in your life and not let history dictate the rest of your life."

So, as you can see, Vinnie, my past choices have placed me where I am today. Herb didn't just advise me to start a new chapter in my life; he suggested that I write a whole new book. The irony of his guidance is that I did just that. Metaphorically and literally I wrote a new book. Vinnie smiled slightly and reached for the conference program and, as he opened it, said thoughtfully, "Your presentation today is entitled Making a Difference. How exactly can a person make a difference?"

That is a question I will answer about 90 minutes from now. Please contact your supervisor and ask that person to meet us backstage. "That is correct," Vinnie acknowledged. "Mr. Gilliland would like you to meet us backstage in five minutes." It seemed an eternity but, finally, Vinnie heard his superior say, "Mr. Gilliland, how may I assist you?" Turning to Vinnie's supervisor, I said, "Would you please permit Vinnie to attend my presentation?" For a moment, I could see the puzzlement on his face until he answered, "I don't think that should be a problem since, after all, his job is to assist you." And with that, Vinnie's boss exited stage left (pun intended) and Vinnie excitedly anticipated his front row seat.

1

TURN THE PAGE

You may not always make right decisions;

however, you have the ability

to make a decision

and then make it right.

TURN THE PAGE

S o how does a small town Pennsylvania boy go from being broke at age 39 to building a seven-figure business by age 50? I turned the page! And the best way to do that is to objectively review the conclusions you've drawn about life. Any conclusion you've drawn that isn't working for you could be working against you. The best way to counteract misinformation and wrong data is to input new and accurate information. Don't squander time being angry about the circumstances you're in. Be curious about how you got there. If I would have invested as much time and energy discovering what I did wrong in my first marriage as I did trying to point out all of her shortcomings, I would have rapidly realized the situation I was in was of my own choosing. Not until I accepted responsibility for my past and stopped blaming my present situation on everyone but myself, did I realize that my history would not control my future.

DON'T SQUANDER TIME BEING ANGRY ABOUT
THE CIRCUMSTANCES YOU'RE IN. BE CURIOUS
ABOUT HOW YOU GOT THERE.

It was time to focus on the future and improve myself. Your potential lies ahead of you regardless of your age. You can become better tomorrow than you are today, but it requires letting go of your past and learning from success and failure. The information you need to gather is from your personal experience. If you're doing something wrong, evaluate what you are doing wrong and be willing to change things to make it right.

MAKE PEACE WITH YOURSELF

As you begin new chapters in your life, ask yourself some questions: What are my goals and objectives? What is my plan to get there? What do I have to become skilled in and what do I need to modify in order to make myself proficient in meeting the expectations of my life? While I cannot tell you precisely how to answer those questions, I can share what worked best for me. Too many people try to turn the page without letting go of the regrets from previous chapters in their life. Regret is a tough feeling to leave behind. It preoccupies you in ways that will demoralize you and your ability to let go of the past and improve your future. Anytime you look back you can recall several things you wish you would have done differently. The key is to keep these things in perspective and accept them as an inevitable part of growth.

REGRET PREOCCUPIES YOU IN WAYS THAT WILL DEMORALIZE YOU AND YOUR ABILITY TO LET GO OF THE PAST AND IMPROVE YOUR FUTURE.

I had many misgivings about several aspects of my life, especially the role I played with my sons during their adolescent years. However, it doesn't help much to dwell on the things I did or didn't do in the past. At the time, I did the very best I could, given my knowledge and experience. I did not do anything deliberately to let my sons down even though some of my good intentions might have been applied incorrectly. Now having two stepsons, I have come to terms with my past mistakes and accepted them as pointers from which I have learned some helpful lessons. Since you can't go back and undo past mistakes, why dwell on them and become obsessed? This will unavoidably affect your family, friends, career and every other aspect of your life?

TURN OUT THE LIGHTS AND TAKE INVENTORY

Do you remember when Don Meredith was part of the broadcast team for *Monday Night Football*? Besides dating yourself as I just did, you will smile at the remembrance of the song he would sing at the end of the game, "the party's over." When "Dandy" Don Meredith began to sing and indicate to the spectators the game might as well end now even though several minutes remained, he was basically saying, "It's over and time to move on to the next game." The certainty of any circumstance can disclose a fact that will not permit you to wholly believe it and this ultimately directs you to repeat the same mistakes. We have an intrinsic sense that if we do the same thing, on a different day, it may turn out differently. We read the same page hoping it has changed since the last time we examined it. When you conclude "the party is over" it is time for you to be honest with yourself. As you read in my introduction, my counselor challenged me to embrace the situation and most importantly, be honest with myself.

THE CERTAINTY OF ANY CIRCUMSTANCE CAN DISCLOSE A FACT THAT WILL NOT PERMIT YOU TO WHOLLY BELIEVE IT AND THIS ULTIMATELY DIRECTS YOU TO REPEAT THE SAME MISTAKES.

You need to honestly face the tough questions and realize where you are, how you got there, and who you have impacted along the way. Being willing to ask the tough question isn't the hard part. It is having the guts to answer the question honestly. It is about ascertaining who you are, or as some counselors suggest, taking time to discover yourself. For almost 40 years of my life I, in fact, believed I needed to be someone else. In an attempt to climb the ladder professionally and socially, I never exposed the real me. My goal was always to be what I perceived other people wanted me to be and, moreover, what I perceived true success to be. For me, it was all about being liked and having people accept as true something that wasn't. Even when I struggled financially, I continued to "pick up the tab" at a restaurant just to impress the people I was with. Furthermore, I was trouncing who I truly was to please my mother and my in-laws. As strict Christians, they both shared strong opinions habitually regarding any lifestyle that didn't fit their view of Christianity. Not that their views were wrong, but they were their views, not mine.

BEING WILLING TO ASK THE TOUGH QUESTION ISN'T THE HARD PART. IT IS HAVING THE GUTS TO ANSWER THE QUESTION HONESTLY.

As a substitute for taking stock of who I was and living that life, I determined it was easier to let my bold nature turn into untrustworthiness which would eventually lead me down disparaging paths. I hastily set aside everything that was important to me and became undisciplined in every aspect of my life. When I finally hit the wall, everything that meant anything to me had vanished. My family, friends and livelihood were all gone. It was then, and only then, that I began to do some soul searching and answer the tough questions I needed to ask myself. My longing was to have power over of my state of affairs, but I didn't know how.

SEIZE CONTROL OF YOUR EGO

How we think and how we respond has a far greater capacity to tear down our lives than any challenge we face. How quickly we respond to misfortune is far more important than adversity itself. The greatest challenge of life is to be in command of the process of our own thinking. We all have experienced distress, misery and heartbreak, but why do people arrive at such diverse places at the end of the journey? Ego! It gets in the way and seats us in our current circumstances. Not until we begin to live a life based on who we are, will we ever truly accomplish what we are capable of. If you want to make a difference, you have to merge your ego (personality) with the aspiration of your soul. In spite of our best efforts, we have moments when things just seem to fall apart. It is during these times that you must be true to who you are and allow your soul and not your ego to steer you. Here are six distinct differences between your ego and your soul to help you comprehend why they can be a counterproductive force if not fused within your inner self.

EGO	SOUL
Reactive	Creative
Driven by fear	Centered in peace
Lives in the past	Lives in destiny
About surviving	About the journey (Enjoy The Ride!)
Focuses on what's wrong	Looks for meaning
Low trust in others	Has faith in others

If there was ever an epiphany in my life, it was when I discovered that my ego was in command of my soul. The discovery process to finding the real Steve was not just a turning point that would shape my life, but it would become an intricate part of my personal and professional beliefs today. When I realized who I was and, more importantly, who I most wanted to be, my life changed in a foremost way. Then, and only then, was I truly capable of making a difference.

DISCOVER WHO YOU ARE

Counselors implore people to discover themselves. In doing so, they inquire about what it is that makes life worthwhile for us? They also want us to outline where we want to go and what we are yearning to see. Questions about our income, where we want to live and how we feel about ourselves are all part of the discovery process. Where do you see yourself five years from now? Who will be a part of your life and play a major role in it five years from now? Are the people who are currently in your inner circle of friends helping you or hurting you? All great questions that when answered will help you better know yourself. However, the number one question that needs to be answered first: Who are you? Tom Voccola introduced the following exercise to me and it served as a powerful tool in determining who I really was. I would encourage you to use a separate sheet of paper and take a few minutes to complete the following exercise.

Make a list of seven people for whom you have a high regard. Beside each name, list the attributes and qualities you most admire in them. The attributes and qualities do not necessarily need to be limited to one word answers. However, the more succinct the words, the easier it will be to analyze your answers.

PERSON	ATTRIBUTE/QUALITY	ATTRIBUTE/QUALITY	ATTRIBUTE/QUALITY
Mom	Honesty	Clever	Smart
Jim	Unconditional Love	Good listener	
Megan	Passion	Thoroughness	
Ron	Passion	Smart	
Brock	Laugh/Smile		Forgiving
Beth	Humor	Bluntness	Political Saavy

Now that you have finished the exercise, it is time to uncover the real you. These lists are a direct reflection of you and, most importantly, represent who you really are or, just as importantly, who you desire to be. Circle any patterns or themes that emerged in the twenty-one attributes/qualities that you listed. You should notice on your chart several words or similar words that are listed more than once. These words unveil a lot about who you really are or aspire to be. You possibly will discover that a common characteristic you admire in another person is something you see as a deficiency in yourself. As you strive to *make a difference,* you will need to determine three things about yourself. What attribute do you admire in other people that you need to improve? What qualities do you possess, that when faced with adversity, tend to take a backseat to your ego? What characteristics about yourself are steadfast and give people a glimpse of who you really are?

COMMON CHARACTERISTICS YOU ADMIRE IN OTHER PEOPLE ARE SOMETHING YOU SEE AS A DEFICIENCY IN YOURSELF.

Who are you? More importantly, who do you want to be? How much disparity is there between who you, in fact, are and who your family, friends and colleagues see you as? The time is now for you to unite your ego with the ambition of your soul and begin an evolution of improvement to becoming who you truly are. When you admire people for a set of values you want but don't possess, you must commit yourself to being that person and be the difference maker you were intended to be.

STAY WITHIN YOURSELF

Everything you think you require to be successful is in your life already. When your ego interrupts who you really are, your tendency is to chase after things outside of you to find fulfillment. You chase money, fame, material possessions and experiences that never fill you up completely. Your focus shifts to being the person your ego drives you to believe will be more received by people. Ironically, you begin to attract who you are (or in this case are not) and when the real you emerges, there is a colossal variance between the true you and the people you have attracted. All too often the "hidden you" is never allowed to surface and you live a segment of your life playing a character frantically trying to be accepted.

MAKING A DIFFERENCE REQUIRES YOU TO MERGE YOUR EGO WITH THE ASPIRATION OF YOUR SOUL.

From grade school, through high school, all I wanted was to be accepted as one of the "cool" kids in school. I did everything and anything to be that guy, but regrettably was never true to myself. As a young adult I rotated between my ego and my soul. The generous, caring, loyal person I am was too often overrun by my selfishness, insensitivity and mistrust. Those who knew me well could only wonder why my actions didn't match my beliefs. The good news is that regardless of who we pretend to be, the real us is still sheathed within and when released allows us to discover so many things that were already a part of us. The Steve Gilliland that family, friends and acquaintances had come to know, would cause a hesitancy regarding whether or not they thought I was capable of changing (turning the page). More often than I care to remember, all I heard was, "we'll see." While it didn't take place overnight, I am pleased to have discovered who I truly am and live within myself, being the person God intended me to be.

HANG IN THERE

Endurance is the restrained side of perseverance. The Serenity Prayer cautions us to focus our efforts on what we can change and accept what we cannot. "When external circumstances rain on our parade, patience is our umbrella. Instead of blaming what we cannot control, patience gives us pause for reflection so we can dry off and start looking for the sun to come out. Everything over time is either ongoing or off going," says Dennis Waitley. You can't undo everything overnight. It took me the better part of a decade to reach the point of where I am at today and, for what it's worth, it wasn't easy. A clear picture of what you should do with the rest of your life may not surface anytime soon. Even when I took responsibility for my situation, the situation was real and continued to be a part of my life. The bills didn't stop arriving in my mailbox and I was about to be out of work. To make matters worse, I would be in constant view of the people I once tried to impress, only to have them sneer, deride and mock my failures. When I attended my son's high school sporting events, it was a feeding frenzy for these people.

FOCUS YOUR EFFORTS ON WHAT YOU CAN CHANGE AND ACCEPT WHAT YOU CANNOT.

My solution was to be determined and endure the new ride regardless of how long it would take and how many obstacles I would encounter. There is no step-by-step system that guarantees everything turns out right. The foremost predicament occurs whenever the new blueprint doesn't work quite the way you envisioned, you get disheartened and start going backwards instead of forward. Prior to meeting my wife, Diane, there were some major barriers regarding my post-divorce relationships that caused me to go in reverse and revisit my past. Naturally, people who had judged me before were in the front row to say, "I told you he wouldn't change." Realize that when you get in unfamiliar territory, it may take some practice before you get it right. This isn't the end of the world, it is simply what it is. Eventually you will find your way and regain control of your life if you are unrelenting. Time changes everything and with persistence, we can keep the passion that fuels us reasonably unvarying. If we can just hang on long enough, time will create for us conditions that allow us to succeed and make a difference.

BE COURAGEOUS

At some point while turning the page you hopefully will be ready to become what you are intended to be. In conflict will be your old personality still trying to please and impress everyone. Regardless of where you are, who is a part of your life and how unappealing the future may appear, the next pages of your life can be enriching and fulfilling. However, from time to time, we are disinclined to change anything about our lives because we enjoy the reassurance of familiarity. The courage to broaden your horizons takes more than a desire to change. It requires a motivation to change with the realization that, if you don't, your passage may fall short given your opposition to transforming.

Not convinced? Look at a global example. Frared Zederia, in his book *Post American War* points out, "The tallest building in the world is now in Taipei, and it will soon be overtaken by one being built in Dubai. The world's richest man is Mexican and its largest publicly traded corporation is Chinese. The world's biggest plane is built in Russia and Ukraine, its leading refinery is under construction in India. The world's largest ferris wheel is in Singapore. The world's number one casino is not in Las Vegas, but in Macao." Although these lists may not seem important to you personally, they serve to remind us, on a much larger scale, that change is inevitable, our growth is optional. It takes courage to make a difference!

As I turned the page in my life, I walked down an abandoned path. My mother, brother (my only sibling), and everyone else who was a part of my life disappeared for a period of time. My father in no way had a significant role in my life, my mother was disappointed in where I had landed because of my choices and my brother was more or less blissfully content with my circumstances. I was an embarrassment to my family and my "so called" friends were all gone with the exception of one – my best friend to this very day, Todd Crissman. While people questioned his motives and advised him to distance himself from me, he nonetheless continued to support me and remained a true friend. With my faith in people devastated, it was Todd's unconditional acceptance that proved to be the force I needed as I approached unfamiliar circumstances. He always believed that with enough time, thought and positive attitude, you can solve just about anything. And the good news – he was absolutely correct!

KEEP THE FAITH

At my darkest hour, with my theological and doctrinal formulations in question, I never doubted God. I remember thinking that my circumstances weren't something I could wave a magic wand over or dream my way out of, but rather something I could only trust my way out of. I remember saying a prayer, which, in retrospect, was probably the beginning of when I started turning the page. I asked God to forgive me for my choices and help me to make better ones. I also asked Him to give me a second chance. I prayed that my marriage could recover and that anyone I had embarrassed or disappointed would also give me a second chance. God gave me a second chance and, although my wife and her family decided life would be better without me, God's blueprint for my life was already written. I guess when Garth Brooks wrote the song, *Unanswered Prayers*, he had me in mind. The assurance I had was that my prayers were answered in accordance to His will, not mine. I look back from where I am today and marvel at how everything unfolded. It is amazing what happens when you keep the faith and rely solely on God.

ACQUIRE SELECTIVE HEARING

If you are willing to change, everything can and will change for you. One of the reasons people don't do well is because they keep trying to get through the day instead of getting something from the day. Pay attention during your day, watch what's going on and become a good listener. Surround yourself with people you respect and admire. My mother has always preached the same sermon when it comes to relationships, "Surround yourself with a character of people that bear a resemblance to who you want to become." Find people whose personalities and achievements stimulate, fascinate and inspire you and then strive to duplicate their patterns of superiority, or as Mark Victor Hansen has stated from the platform, "duplicate patterns of excellence." You have to monitor and think about what is happening around you. Often the most extraordinary opportunities are hidden among insignificant events. As you listen, be selective. With so many opinions and voices vying for your attention, you have to be discerning and fortify your listening proficiency. If a voice is not leading to the achievement of your goals, exercise caution in how long you listen.

FIND PEOPLE WHOSE PERSONALITIES AND ACHIEVEMENTS STIMULATE, FASCINATE AND INSPIRE YOU AND THEN STRIVE TO DUPLICATE THEIR PATTERNS OF SUPERIORITY.

As a member of the National Speakers Association, I regularly caution new speakers to be judicious in accepting all the direction they hear from their contemporaries. There are an abundance of ideas, volumes of best practices and countless beliefs about how to build a successful speaking business. Nonetheless, what works for one speaker may not work for others. The key is to be aligned with people who are moving in the precise direction you want to go. It is one thing to pronounce you are heading to Pennsylvania. It is an entirely different thing to articulate on whether you want to end up in Pittsburgh or Philadelphia. As you turn the page, be sure to head in the right direction.

BE DISCIPLINED

Every day is filled with dozens of personal crossroads, moments when you're called upon to make decisions regarding minor as well as major questions. These decisions chart a path to a future destination and ultimately determine your happiness and success. With vigilant intellectual preparation, you can make prudent choices. It is essential that you make fitting decisions. Anytime I eat right and exercise, I experience positive results and feel vitality almost immediately. The key – discipline! The same can be said of reading. At a conference I attended, Zig Ziglar challenged the audience to read more and become carnivores of information. When you begin reading, you experience a growing awareness and new level of self-confidence. Granted, some things you already know are said in a different way, but the question is whether or not it affirms what you are doing or reminds you of what you are not doing. New disciplines practiced daily will produce exciting results. Turning the page requires new disciplines that will cause us to amend our thinking.

NAVIGATE THE DETOURS

As you *Enjoy The Ride*™, never forget that your personal and professional journey will always have some detours. Many people who dream of living a successful life never do because they are unwilling to change direction or follow direction. The ultimate outcome of anyone's life is a matter of personal choice. Our thought process is the power behind whether or not we will permit our lives to be motivated by a purpose. To be purpose-driven you have to believe in yourself, be true to yourself, grow yourself, take responsibility for yourself, refocus yourself and change yourself.

When you are at the lowest point in your life and everyone has abandoned their belief in you, never stop believing in yourself. When you believe in yourself, you are better able to focus on improving yourself. When you don't believe in yourself, you expect the worst, not only of yourself, but of others. If you are insecure, you struggle to center on anything but yourself because you are always worried about how you look, what others think about you and whether you're going to fail. Stop worrying about what other people think of you. Why is their opinion of you more important than your own? You will always be restricted when your future depends on the opinion and consent of others. Remember this – if you are afraid of criticism you will depart this life doing nothing.

WHEN YOU DON'T BELIEVE IN YOURSELF, YOU
EXPECT THE WORST, NOT ONLY OF YOURSELF,
BUT OF OTHERS.

You have to *be true to yourself*. When the potholes of life materialize, search for a resolution and fuel your passion to keep the fire burning. It is when you become defensive and hunt for a getaway plan that you reveal that your passion was not genuine. If you are looking for the conditions of any situation to be exactly right, you will struggle to be happy or successful. No matter what the circumstances, positive people see opportunities everywhere. They understand that opportunities aren't based on luck or position. They are realized by preparation and a positive attitude. Unearthing problems doesn't take anything special. What is exceptional, however, is seeing a solution in every problem and a possibility in every difficulty. Opportunity exists where you find it and it always looks bigger going than coming.

It is also essential to surround yourself with people who have negotiated the detours of life and found opportunities in them. Grow yourself by finding a wise person who has accomplished what you wish for in your own life and apply it to your life. Stop rationalizing your actions and pay attention to what they do. Accepting instruction from people is a life-changing choice that will help you break away from your own negative thinking and allow you to grow. Anytime you put up with mediocrity in your choice of acquaintances, you become more comfortable with mediocrity in your own life. Only a fool ignores the leadership of wise people. Charles "Tremendous" Jones said that the only difference between who you are today and the person you will be in five years will come from the books you read and the people with whom you associate.

ACCEPTING INSTRUCTION FROM PEOPLE IS
A LIFE-CHANGING CHOICE THAT WILL HELP
YOU BREAK AWAY FROM YOUR OWN NEGATIVE
THINKING AND ALLOW YOU TO GROW.

Success is limited to people who understand and accept that they are in situations of their own choosing. If your tendency is to say, "It's not my fault," and blame everyone but yourself, the probability of you ever being truly happy and successful is slight. You will forever have a reason or excuse for your current situation and, as expected, you will never see it as your responsibility. Unsuccessful people duck responsibility. Positive and successful people *take responsibility* for their own lives. Your thinking dictates your decisions. Until you accept complete responsibility for your past, you will never be free to move into a brighter future. Allowing your spouse, friends and family to rationalize your behavior only adds difficulty. Accept responsibility for your own problems – it is the beginning of wisdom. Who you are, where you are, and where you will go is your responsibility – so take it!

Think about your situation. Have you ever been wronged? Have there been times when you haven't gotten everything you deserved? Do you spend your time and energy on what should have been or are you going to focus on what can be? Even when truth and justice are on your side, you may never be able to right your wrongs. A major detour in your journey is when you allow destructive emotions to consume your energy and make you negative. As you look backward, trying to right your wrongs, you become resentful, angry, hateful and bitter. Instead of worrying about someone ever making it right, *refocus yourself* so you can move forward. Every mistake, broken promise and slip-up can develop a paralyzing grip. Stop wasting priceless hours envisioning revenge toward an uncaring person. Resentment is about another person who seldom gives thought to their offense. When you grant forgiveness, you release your past and create a new beginning. You can't make any progress when you are going the wrong way. If you want to get around the detours faster, travel light. Remove all the resentment, jealousies, unforgiveness, self-centeredness and reservations from your backpack.

A MAJOR DETOUR IN YOUR JOURNEY IS WHEN
YOU ALLOW DESTRUCTIVE EMOTIONS TO
CONSUME YOUR ENERGY AND
MAKE YOU NEGATIVE.

You may not possess the ability to always make right decisions. However, you do hold the ability to make a decision and then make it right. You can change your future by *changing yourself.* Change requires action. It all comes down to this. There will come a time in your life when you will face a detour and a decision is required. And that decision and how you make it will have a far-reaching effect on generations unborn. Happiness and success are not the same for everyone because their meanings are different for every person. But the ultimate outcome of anyone's life will always be determined by their ability to navigate the detours.

LET THEM WALK

The hardest part of turning the page concerns people – people who were a part of your past but ostensibly vanished when the challenging times materialized; people you treated like relatives and considered as friends who simply walked out of your life to go a different direction. I would have never predicted that certain people would have walked away from me. The struggle I had was letting them walk. My counselor, Herb, always said, "Don't try to talk your wife into staying with you, loving you, calling you, caring about you, coming to see you, staying attached to you. If she can walk away from you, let her walk. Your destiny will not be tied to anyone who is willing to walk out of your life." The Bible says, "They came out from us that it might be made manifest that they were not for us. For had they been of us, no doubt they would have continued with us." [1 John 2:19]

YOUR DESTINY WILL NOT BE TIED TO ANYONE WHO IS WILLING TO WALK OUT OF YOUR LIFE.

It doesn't mean they are a bad person. It just means their part in the story is over. The rough part is the ability to comprehend when a person's part in your story is over so that you don't keep trying to revive something that is forever departed. You've got to know when it's over. It took me a long time to acquire the gift of goodbye. I know whatever God means for me to have, He'll give to me. If it takes too much fret and worry, I usually don't need it. The day I officially starting turning the page in my life was the day I stop petitioning people to stay and simply let them go!

LET GO AND LET GOD

In order to turn the page you need to let go if you are holding on to something that doesn't belong to you and was never intended for your life. As the saying goes, "We can't appreciate a butterfly if we keep it in our hands. We have to let it fly to enjoy it. If the rain comes and it flies back to us, it's ours to keep." If you are holding on to past hurts and pains, let go. If someone can't treat you right, love you back and see your worth, let go. If someone has angered you, let go. If you are holding on to some thoughts of evil and revenge, let go. If you are involved in a wrong relationship or dependence, let go. If you are holding on to a job that no longer meets your needs or abilities, let go. If you have a dire attitude, let go. If you keep judging others to make yourself feel better, let go. If you're stuck in the past and God is trying to take you to a new level, let Him take you there.

YOU CAN'T CHANGE YESTERDAY, BUT YOU CAN
RUIN TODAY BY WORRYING
ABOUT TOMORROW.

If you are struggling with the healing of a broken relationship, let go. If you keep trying to help someone who won't even try to help themselves, let go. If you're feeling depressed and stressed, let go. Take responsibility for your past, start a new chapter and let go. You can't change yesterday, but you can ruin today by worrying about tomorrow. Instead of reading the same page over and over, it is time for you to turn the page. It is time to start a new chapter in your life and not let history dictate the rest of your life.

CHAPTER AFTERTHOUGHT

As you turn the page, consider...

- ❖ There are at least two people in this world that you would die for.

- ❖ At least 15 people in this world love you in some way.

- ❖ The only reason anyone would ever hate you is because they want to be just like you.

- ❖ A smile from you can bring happiness to anyone, even if they don't like you.

- ❖ Every night someone thinks about you before they go to sleep.

- ❖ You mean the world to someone.

- ❖ You are special and unique.

- ❖ When you make the biggest mistake ever, something good comes from it.

- ❖ When you think the world has turned its back on you, take another look.

- ❖ Someone that you don't even know exists admires you.

2

LIVE YOUR
OWN DESTINY

It is better to live your own destiny

imperfectly than to live an

imitation of somebody else's

life with perfection.

LIVE YOUR
OWN DESTINY

If you could go anywhere, where would you like to go? Not in terms of vacations, but in your life. Your answer to that question does a lot to determine whether or not you'll make a difference during your lifetime. We are all on a journey and, while the true joy of life is in the trip, the real question is who is in command of your voyage. Letting others determine your destiny is like boarding a plane headed to nowhere and then complaining about where you land. You have a choice to fulfill your purpose and grow toward your potential by living your own destiny.

Most of us will never receive a gold medal, Emmy, Pulitzer or the Heisman Trophy award. Conversely, we can make choices that will provide us with the opportunity to enjoy the ride and afford all that was meant for us. As you will read later, our lives are full of potential, but many people experience only a portion of life's potential because they haven't decided what they want or where their life is going. "I just want to live day by day and see what happens" is a common approach to life. Quality of life does not happen by chance. A fulfilling life begins with searching for and clarifying our reason for living...our life's purpose.

WE CAN MAKE CHOICES THAT WILL PROVIDE US
WITH THE OPPORTUNITY TO ENJOY THE RIDE
AND AFFORD ALL THAT WAS MEANT FOR US.

Imagine for a moment that at your 50th high school class reunion the organizers are going to print a far-reaching story outlining your personal and professional achievements. How would you want them to describe to your classmates what you had achieved? What would you want contemporaries to say about you? What would you tell them was your primary purpose in life? Purpose describes the kind of business our life is in and what we are living for. A meaningful purpose communicates what you want to accomplish and the contributions you want to make. Your purpose is what you want to become – the person and character you desire to be, not someone else's plan. Making a difference is about what you believe to be important and what gives meaning to your daily actions. Purpose is about your future and the one-of-a-kind journey you seek to live.

THE DISCOVERY PROCESS

My stepson Adam is in the midst of his final year of college. Since his senior year in high school, he has vacillated about what he will do upon graduation. He is a bright young man who has always been drawn to music. An excellent drummer, Adam has taught himself to also play the piano, guitar, mandolin, banjo and ukulele. He is outwardly the happiest when music is a part of his day and he is perpetually practicing to improve his skills. Not surprising, he will graduate with a double major. The astonishing part to many people is that Adam's two majors are German and History. As you might expect, every time we discuss his future, the frustration is evident. Yes, he enjoys the challenge of learning the German language. Yes, he is fascinated by world history, but his earnest passion is music.

FIND YOUR PURPOSE. DEFINE IT AND MAKE IT THE CORE OF WHAT DRIVES YOU.

I believe that each of us has a dream deep inside that speaks to the very essence of who we are meant to be. It's the thing we were born to do. It draws on our God-given abilities. So why do so many people abandon their heartfelt dream? Just like Adam, their dreams are very easily broken because of the urgency to earn a paycheck to pay for the apartment, car, insurance, student loans and a lifestyle which they have chosen. Too many people chose a path early in life that inevitably creates a lifestyle instead of producing their own destiny. Why? The answer is our incapacity to unearth our purpose in life and the easiness to replicate what society and family say is our destiny.

LIVE BY DESIGN

You decide! Without any effort on our part, we allow circumstances and others to dictate to us the major decisions of our lives and thus determine who we are and what we will become. We let others define and, in some cases, limit our potential to be successful. We merely go with the flow, synchronized and directed by others, undaunted about where we are going. It's time to take charge and live by your blueprint. The people who will tell you it can't be done will always get their paychecks signed by those who say it can be done. Have you ever dreamed about signing the front of your paycheck instead of the back? Let your imagination wander freely across the landscape of all possibilities resting on those that might become probabilities, and eventually choosing those that you desire to pursue into reality.

WE LET OTHERS DEFINE, AND IN SOME CASES, LIMIT OUR POTENTIAL TO BE SUCCESSFUL.

Think bigger today than you did 10 years ago. Dare to reignite the dreams that once filled your every thought. Don't be content with mediocrity or else your inclination will be to waste a lifetime and then someday look back and say, "If only I had," or "I wonder what might have been." Unless you rise above your state of affairs, you will never see the world for what it could be. You will replay the same scenarios, worries and ideas. Before you know it, your inner circle of friends will be a sounding board for your commonplace anxiety for meaningless matters, pointless chitchat and, worse yet, gossip.

By my 50th birthday, my thought process was way ahead of my thinking when I was 40. When I was in my early 40's, I was always doing fine under the circumstances. By the time I hit 50, I was out from under my circumstances because I made a conscious choice to live by design – my own design! I was open to ideas, new situations and new challenges. I was growing and evolving and seeing a part of the world I had only ever dreamed about. I was on my way enjoying the beauty, drama and joy that was a part of my own design. Sure, painting by numbers was easier, but when I grabbed hold of a blank canvas and started painting my own destiny, it was so much more exciting and, more importantly, much more rewarding.

DREAM BIG

Hilary Swank was a teenager when her mom packed her up and headed to Hollywood. They had $75, a Mobil card and no place to live when they got there. They lived in a car for a few weeks and then slept on the floor of a friend's house. Homeless, but never hopeless, Hilary began landing small parts. Her break came in 1999 with the starring role for *Boys Don't Cry*, which earned her an Oscar for best actress. "I'm just a girl from a trailer park who had a dream," she said at the Academy Awards. In 2005, with *Million Dollar Baby*, she became one of a few actresses to ever receive two Academy Awards. It wouldn't have happened if not for the dream and the drive to pursue it. She was lucky enough to have a mom who said she could be anything in life.

A DREAM WILL PROVIDE YOU WITH A REASON TO GO, A PATH TO FOLLOW AND A TARGET TO HIT.

If you have detoured from the path of a long-term dream you once held close to your heart, explore what it would take to pursue that dream at this point in your life. It may not be impossible to get back on track. Are you so busy struggling with the day-to-day grinds that you are rarely thinking about what lies ahead? As you daydream, have you been selling yourself short in one or more areas of your life? Are you allowing other people to censor your imaginings and goals? Is there more you could be doing in one part of your life, but fear keeps you from pursuing it? Are you living up to what you could be? Do you have a keen awareness of the future? If you haven't already discovered your dream, you're probably realizing how much you've been missing.

A dream will provide you with a reason to go, a path to follow and a target to hit. Wouldn't you say it's about time you get started?

Dreams should never expire. They visualize a better future, happier day-to-day life, more fulfilling work, more fulfilling relationships and deeper, lasting joy. Dreams are about hopefulness and the capability for you to break away from the restrictions that mediocre thinking has imprisoned within you. Most dreams are worth dreaming and pursuing. When you begin to dream, picture the worst-case scenario and the paramount ending. Even as you appraise your vision for your own destiny, don't let anyone or anything deflate it. Your dreams and goals may not be clearly in the scope of your reach but, with enough fortitude, the dream that once seemed so big can someday be your reality.

SURVIVE THE CRITICS

Success is attained in inches, not miles. However, because of the demands to succeed by the world's meaning, we abandon our purpose and leap forward to satisfy our attackers. People who should be encouragers offering up a healthy dosage of "you can do it" are too often donating unwanted disparagement. Close friends and family members offer up a huge amount of opinion which is usually connected to monetary goals. Their scrutiny is strictly based on what they believe will bring you happiness – financial security. Since they are close to you, they are usually the only people who know about your dreams, goals and plans. You can weather the criticism of a stranger, but you have a harder time surviving when your dreams are diluted by a loved one. While they want to help you, they can also hinder you. Your dreams are your dreams to go after and if you truly believe they are your destiny, then you have to endure the speculative analysis and go full speed ahead.

SUCCESS IS ATTAINED IN INCHES, NOT MILES.

DeShea Townsend, the former all-pro cornerback for the Super Bowl Champion Pittsburgh Steelers retired from football recently and made contact with me regarding my profession as a speaker and author. At our initial breakfast, I asked DeShea a question about his purpose in life. "If you had never made it to the NFL, what would you have done?" I asked. "Teaching!" he responded with decisiveness and confidence. He went on to say that his goal in life was to impact people, especially young people. He felt that a good path to pursue was professional speaking where he could use his NFL career as a platform to influence people with his message. "When you are 5'9" and weigh 155 pounds, you are told too often what you can't do and are rarely encouraged to discover your purpose and pursue your passion. For me, I loved playing football and always believed I could play at the most elite level. I never let my detractors and critics get in the way of my dreams. Fortunately, my mother and father were my biggest supporters and they, too, had to survive the critics."

As I finished my senior year of high school, my mother was intent on me being a minister or something connected with the church. Because of her steadfast desire for me to have a career that would optimize her Christianity and her outspoken opinion, I attended a Christian college for my freshman and sophomore years. Without declaring a major, I placed my dream of writing and some day owning my own business on hold. By the time I would graduate, I was married with a wife and two children. By my 22nd birthday, my dreams were like a bubble in a room full of pins with the fan blowing. Add to that, I was surrounded by people who no matter what I was for, they were against. The people who wanted to help me be successful in pursuing my passion were few and far between. Fortunately, I possessed the tenacity and commitment to follow my fervor and, almost 20 years later, turned my dream into a reality. For Adam, it will be a tough choice, but nonetheless his choice. Although his love is music, he may not follow a career which allows him to capitalize on that love. The invariable demands from the outside world and everyone's distorted view of success may cause him to steer away from what is undoubtedly his passion and life calling. I may be wrong, but you only need to monitor his spare time to realize that young man has a gift which isn't bestowed upon everyone. You can only become truly accomplished at something you love. Maya Angelou, poet, author and speaker said, "Don't make money your goal. Instead, pursue the things you love doing, and then do them so well that people can't take their eyes off of you."

ENDURE THOSE WITH A KNACK

Lucy, of Peanuts cartoon fame, is renowned for her critical and caustic comments. On one occasion, she told Charlie Brown, "You are the foul ball in the line drive of life." In another strip, Linus had his security blanket in place and his thumb resting safely in his mouth, but he was troubled. Turning to Lucy, who was sitting next to him, he asked, "Why are you always so anxious to criticize me?" The response was typical Lucy, "I just think I have a knack for seeing other people's faults." Exasperated, Linus threw up his hands and asked, "What about your own faults?" Without hesitation, Lucy explained, "I have a knack for overlooking them." Lucy is not the only one who believes their knack or calling in life is to point out and correct the weaknesses of others. Unfortunately, these same people are customarily blind to their own shortcomings. It might be wise for those who possess their self-proclaimed gift of criticism to consider the wise words of Frank A.

Clark, "Lots of faults we think we see in others are simply the ones we expect to find there because we have them."

BE PATIENT

How does patience relate to the deep desire to find a destiny worthy of ourselves? It is absolutely indispensable! According to Anne Wilson Schaef, "No one can attain the fullness of his or her whole life without acquiring it early in life or according to a timetable. No one can find a destiny worthy of a full life without living that full life conscientiously, passionately and in the natural order it occurs. When we plant a flower or a tree, we need to have the patience to let it grow and the same is true of ourselves. As long as we are persistent in our pursuit of our deepest destiny, we will continue to grow. We cannot choose the day or time when we will bloom fully. It will happen in its own time."

DEVELOP CONSTRUCTIVE DISSATISFACTION

When you are frustrated and discontent with your position in life, you then, and only then, consider turning the page. As you learned in the previous chapter, you may have made choices you regret, but you have the ability to make them right. Every invention registered in the United States Patent Office is the result of constructive dissatisfaction. Every inventor, not satisfied with something as it was, found a way to create something new and make it better. Even after failures, rejections and bankruptcies, you can still make a difference.

"ALL OUR DREAMS CAN COME TRUE, IF WE HAVE THE COURAGE TO PURSUE THEM."

The man behind the mouse had his share of setbacks while building his Walt Disney empire. Classic films such as *Pinocchio, Bambi* and *Fantasia* failed at the box office in first release and competing studio executives poached Disney's characters and animators. But Disney is an entrepreneur's case study in constructive dissatisfaction and resilience. Despite many failures, the animator kept his nearly obsessed focus on building his growing movie studio, making quality animated films and ultimately creating "the happiest place on earth," Disneyland in California.

CHECK YOUR MOTIVATION

Purpose is the force that rules our lives. Without it, we labor in a profession but never put together a career or find our calling. Without purpose, work becomes a necessary interruption between weekends. Weekends, to many people, are a getaway from a weekly reformatory of insignificance. The success of an effort depends not so much on the outcome of the effort, but on the motive for making the effort in the first place. The motive makes the difference.

Someone once told me, "Never chase money." Chase your passion and the money will follow you." When I built our company, my philosophy was that if we took care of people, the business would follow and so would the revenue. And it did! The greatest men and women in all walks of life who have made the biggest difference did so by expressing something within themselves that had to be expressed. They took the skills and talents they were blessed with and, instead of playing it safe, embarked on a mission to fulfill their life's destiny. Granted, many of these people earned a great deal of money and prestige for what they accomplished, but the key to their success was to be found in the fact that they were motivated more by providing excellence in a product or service to fill a need than by thinking of profit. As I write this paragraph I am listening to *Nikki's Song* on my Bose headset smiling about what lies ahead for Adam. I may not know where his talents in music and patience for teaching himself and others may lead him, but if he can endure the disbelievers, I firmly believe he will be successful and make a huge difference during his lifetime.

LOOK TO CONTRIBUTE

Truly successful individuals look to contribute, not to receive. At the end of this book, I list the top 10 most benevolent people. These people are all driven by a purpose, are passionate about their visions and take pride in everything they do. The employees who love their mission and their work get the raises and promotions more often than the employees who care the most about getting the raises and promotions. People who make a difference don't look for achievements that will bring them the most with the least amount of effort. They look for the challenges that will mean the most to overcome. They do not seek get-rich-quick schemes, lottery jackpots or pyramid fads. They look for something difficult, some problem to solve – the accomplishment of which will give them great personal satisfaction.

PEOPLE WHO MAKE A DIFFERENCE DON'T
LOOK FOR ACHIEVEMENTS THAT WILL BRING
THEM THE MOST WITH THE LEAST
AMOUNT OF EFFORT.

Many people have confided in me that they don't have the vaguest idea about their purpose in life. They lack a spiritual connection and are not open to looking beyond their mortality for meaning. For them,

I simply offer the idea that they can begin to ascertain their purpose through gaining wisdom, experiencing everything possible and sharing the most value they possibly can with other human beings. Any time you make life easier for one person, you give meaning to your existence. As famed author and speaker, Zig Ziglar, states, "If you help enough other people get what they want, you will always get what you want." Our friends, Jason and Brandy Rosenberger, have often expressed to my wife and I how generous we are. They have commented on more than a few occasions that they are overwhelmed by what we have done for other people. So why do we do it? There is always another opportunity to learn, to grow and to extend our reach to someone groping for our strength. I have never been a person to stand on the sideline and be content. Whether it is helping a fellow passenger stow their luggage on a flight, assisting an elderly gentleman get his arm through the sleeve of his jacket or merely smiling and asking the person beside me, "Hello, how is your day going?" Anytime you add value to a situation, you are making a difference.

A JOB, CAREER OR CALLING

In an interview on a morning radio station in Iowa I was asked, "How did you get into professional speaking as your career?" Without time to collect my thoughts, I proceeded to tell my story. On April 16, 1999, on a flight from Pittsburgh, Pennsylvania to Houston, Texas, all I could think about was my first "official" speaking engagement. For the previous fourteen weeks, I had delivered numerous presentations in front of hundreds of people, but those dates were all contracted through a public seminar company. Now it was just me in front of a client who felt my message needed to be shared with her leadership team. I received my first signed program agreement and a check that would be made out to my newly formed S corporation from not just any client, but a Fortune 500 client. The reporter then asked, "Has the economy affected your career and how are you personally handling these tough times?" Despite unprecedented economic instability, I proudly responded that my confirmed bookings for 2010 were ahead of the previous year. As for the tough times, I let him know that you can't help but wish all the hassle would just go away, but that hard times were also a time to look for opportunities.

CHOOSE A JOB YOU LOVE AND YOU WILL NEVER HAVE TO WORK A DAY IN YOUR LIFE.

After the interview, I was disappointed with my answers and immediately realized why. Professional speaking wasn't my career. It was my *calling*. As for the economy, it had no influence on something I'd do even if I weren't paid to do it. And regarding the tough times, this was a chance for me to share *how* previous tough times were actually good for me. Among people who work, some have jobs, some have careers and some have a calling. A calling is inherently rewarding regardless of compensation. And it turns out that finding your calling leads to more success. When you love to do something, you'll do it longer, you'll invest your own money in doing it, you'll do it when you're tired and you'll do it when attractive distractions are available. More than one person has said that you should choose a job you love and you will never have to work a day in your life. We all want and need to be able to pay our bills, but think about where you are in your life. Do all the expensive toys keep you working way too many hours at your job and does the need to bask in your glories keep you hard at work in your career? I've long said that if you won the lottery, how you spent the money and your time would answer a lot of questions about who you are and whether or not you have a job, a career or a calling.

As I celebrated my 52nd birthday and my 12th anniversary of speaking professionally, I spent some time reminiscing about where I've been, where I'm at and where I'm heading. I remembered my first *job* at a car wash, my *career* at a greeting card company and now my *calling* as a professional speaker. I remembered the good times and the tough times. The good times make you smile and the tough times make you thankful. Even in the midst of a recession with all the uncertainty, these harsh times can still bring personal and professional growth. Just like you, I am human and wish we didn't have to go through them, but it is times like these that equip us for the future. William Allen White said, "I am not afraid of tomorrow for I have seen yesterday."

THE GOOD TIMES MAKE YOU SMILE AND THE TOUGH TIMES MADE YOU THANKFUL.

I can unequivocally guarantee you that tough times help you test your limits and, in most cases, allow you to exceed them. In my book, *Mum's The Word*, I talk about the wisdom to *accept life on life's terms* realizing that experience is a hard teacher because it gives you the test first and the lessons afterward. An economist recently stated, "The employment rate was at 91%." When he said it, I thought I misunderstood until he talked about perspective. A wise person once said, "The art of being wise is the art of knowing what to overlook." If we could all apply that in life, we wouldn't suffer from all the self-induced stress caused by worrying about things we can't control or that may never happen. Tough times allow you to reexamine your life's work and your calling. It helps you understand where you are in life and gives you time to reflect on what is really important. You learn to disregard the trivial and focus your attention on what's important. Hard-hitting times abruptly ask the question, "Are you ready?" Twelve years ago I pursued my calling. Being in the right place at the right time is meaningless unless you are ready. George Burns once said, "Whatever you are ready for normally shows up." I was ready to move from a career to a calling when the opportunity was staring me in the face even though the circumstances (tough times) were not my choosing.

TOUGH TIMES ALLOW YOU TO REEXAMINE YOUR LIFE'S WORK AND YOUR CALLING.

How prepared are you for the dream that you desire? Are you focused on the right thing? Do you see these turbulent economic times as a chance to inspire yourself and other people around you and make a real difference? At age 30, I knew in my heart I deserved more than a life of work, work, work so I went from a job to a career. At age 40, I found my calling. Twelve years and counting, I now realize that everything I needed was already there waiting to be discovered.

DESIRE CAN EVEN THE ODDS

What would a book of mine be without a story about a young boy growing up in west Tennessee who just happens to be one of my favorites? He had a burning desire. It appeared, however, his disadvantaged childhood would restrict his dreams. Told that he was from the "wrong side of the tracks," he nonetheless sustained the desire to do and be something special. He had a battered, secondhand guitar but had no idea how to tune or play it. His cousin, country singer Lonzo

Green, came for a visit and met an anxious youngster wanting to learn the guitar. Lonzo took the time to tune the instrument and teach the lad a few basic chords. The boy from the wrong side of the tracks now had something to build his dreams on. In a few short years he turned a slim opportunity into a career that won the hearts of Americans everywhere. Elvis Presley sustained his hunger for music even though the odds were against him. Desire is simply possibility seeking expression even when everything appears against you. More often than not, it is easier to live someone else's definition of you and what they expect than your own. Elvis' pursuit of musical eminence is a historic example of what happens when a craving outlasts the naysayers.

SUSTAIN DON'T COMPLAIN

The lack of persistence is the major reason people never reach their own destiny. Perseverance means doing the tough things first and looking downstream for gratification and rewards. My secretary, Margaret, taught me to always do the thing I liked least first. She said, "You will make more progress and cover more ground when you tackle the tough stuff first. It means being dedicated to always improving and going the extra mile." When I was in sales, it meant making more calls, driving more miles, establishing more contacts, challenging my assumptions, getting up earlier and always being on the lookout for a better way of doing what I was doing. Determination is sticking with something when the odds stack up against you. It is often taking the road least traveled by your family, friends and peers. And, of all the immeasurable advice Margaret gave me, the best may have been after I had come back from attending another pointless meeting with people who talked to hear themselves speak. She said, "Perseverance is not complaining but sustaining."

STOP PROCRASTINATING
AND APPLY EFFORT

Don't expect anyone to do it for you. Some time ago, a foremost magazine had an article that portrayed America as a land of sore losers, spoiled brats, blame fixers, crybabies and victims. In my research for this book, I have come to the realization that people who make a difference do not fall prey to procrastination. If you are prone to play the victim, then you are too concerned about the past and the things you cannot control. Over time, you develop a loser's mindset and affix blame for all your shortcomings when, in reality, it is your lack of exertion and predisposition to put off everything.

PEOPLE WHO MAKE A DIFFERENCE DO NOT
FALL PREY TO PROCRASTINATION.

Victims believe they are always in the wrong place at the wrong time. I could write an entire book on this subject alone. From former co-workers to people who have worked for me, they always have a scapegoat who is the reason for their failures and lack of success. They are experts in excuses. They put their children in private schools, protest when they don't have the money to reimburse the school for past due tuition and then expect someone else to bail them out. They fall behind on their mortgage and yet celebrate Christmas like they don't have a payment in the world. Their glimmer of optimism rests on the phrase *well I guess it could have been worse.* When you discuss their future and possible goals that could help them, there is always someone, or something, keeping them from getting started. Procrastination is motionless disinterest, lack of concern and a lackadaisical attitude. Procrastination overcome, however, moves us into the arena where the law of motion takes over. The first step toward making a difference is the biggest one most people take. That step requires effort. Put forth the same energy to taking the first step instead of making excuses and you will be surprised the difference it makes. As my mother always said, "Once you start, you're half done."

CUT THE CORD

If you are ever going to live your own destiny, you have to become independent of your parental support and cut the cord to experience your own fate. For those of us who have strong-minded mothers and fathers, that is easier written in a book than done. You have to break the dependence to a standard of living you are comfortable with and sometimes take a step backward to move forward. All too often children never dream dreams, set goals or make plans because of the reliance that exists within their immediate family. A parent's opinion, to a child, can sometimes be so intimidating that a move in any direction away from the belief can be viewed as rebellion or lack of respect. *After everything I have done for you* is an all too familiar response from the controlling parent who desires a child to live within the rules of the destiny they have envisioned.

YOU HAVE TO BREAK THE DEPENDENCE TO A
STANDARD OF LIVING YOU ARE COMFORTABLE
WITH AND SOMETIMES TAKE A STEP BACKWARD
TO MOVE FORWARD.

Perhaps the toughest challenge we all face is the jealousy and criticism voiced by family, friends and colleagues. Yes, success has a cost and, if you are going to make a significant difference in your lifetime, the choice to pay the price is a tough one. The fear of that cost keeps many people from pursuing the success that they could enjoy. I am unquestionably not the faultless son and have made my share of blunders. Nonetheless, I will forever be able to state it like Frank Sinatra sang it, "I did it my way."

CHAPTER AFTERTHOUGHT

A few things that make a difference...

❖ Being the anonymous donor

❖ Adopting a 4-legged friend

❖ Saying hi to that person on the bus

❖ Singing in the rain

❖ Handcrafted anything

❖ Leaving early to play with the kids

❖ Taking more photos

❖ Planting a tree

❖ Holding hands

❖ Teaching kids to fish

❖ Having a favorite charity

❖ Volunteering at a shelter

❖ Letting computers sleep

❖ Picnics

❖ Being a mentor

❖ Refusing to fail

❖ Drinking responsibly

❖ Going back to school to teach

❖ Giving compliments

❖ Taking your time

❖ Coaching Little League

❖ Laughing more often

❖ Kissing a boo-boo

❖ Seeing the mug ½ full

❖ Being the tooth fairy

❖ Visiting your childhood home

❖ Falling in love

3

SEIZE THE OPPORTUNITIES

The road to regret

is besieged

with overlooked chances.

SEIZE THE OPPORTUNITIES

In waiting for luck to knock on the front door, we often miss opportunity throwing rocks at our back window. As Mark Sanborn says, "Observe life, look around and pay attention." Opportunity may be knocking. Too many of us are listening for a splendid, beatific voice rather than a simple tug inside our hearts and minds. Opportunity is the fuel that drives the passion which is waiting to burst out of our lives, not seeking to invade us.

Opportunity resides within you and gives you an unsullied way to face each day. It is in the way you think about who you are and what you will do. It's in the way you will perceive the ultimate destiny of your life. It is what fuels you when continuity turns to calamity. The chance to move on from a tough situation isn't something that is advertised through the want ads or purchased in the form of a lottery ticket. Opportunity is a mind-set that ignites the passion within you!

During an extended conversation with a corporate meeting planner who hired me to speak to his employees in Basel, Switzerland, I was informed that a major downsizing had been announced but the details wouldn't be available for at least two months. At some point in the conversation, I shared with him something that had been shared with me when I was going through a challenging time in my life. "Opportunities are literally everywhere, but you won't see any of them unless you first choose within yourself to see them, embrace them and pursue them. You can see the problem resolved and a stronger you emerging from it or you can see it capsizing your life. You can choose to see the need met and you and your family entering a new realm of strength, health, possibilities, wealth and charitable outreach, or you can choose to see the need remaining unmet and consuming your spirit, mind and body as well as those of your family."

OPPORTUNITY IS A MIND SET THAT IGNITES THE PASSION WITHIN YOU!

Each encounter you have every day of your life is an opportunity for you. Each person you meet holds an opportunity for you. Each experience, whether bad or good, is embedded in opportunity. From each encounter, person or experience, you have the opportunity to grow, to learn, to change, to add to your level of awareness, to become more than you presently are and make a difference!

BALANCE IS AN ONGOING PROCESS

Some of us have bought into the illusion that we can work hard to get our lives organized and "balanced" and they will stay that way forever. As I have shared with numerous audiences, we all have a desire to manage our multiple priorities. However, for most of us, we aren't even sure what our priorities are. The two things I am certain of in life are that we can't manage time, we manage the activities that consume our time and we can't achieve total balance. The moment you think you "have it all together," brace yourself because something is lurking around the corner to upset the apple cart. We are trying to balance something that is continuously changing. Anne Wilson Schaef contends, "We are constantly given the opportunity to grow, to learn and to change, but our inability to adapt quickly throws us off balance." She reminds us that "even our automobiles keep trying to teach us that material objects are in a constant state of disintegration, and we don't want to believe that. How much more difficult it is to see ourselves and our world this way."

WE ARE CONSTANTLY GRANTED THE
OPPORTUNITY AND MANDATE TO GROW,
TO LEARN, TO CHANGE.

She believes "balance will never be obtained," and I agree. That isn't a bad thing. It is merely a human stipulation and the way life is. We can either accept it or live with the false notion that it is possible to achieve. "Any aspect of our life that we believe is wholly balanced, that we are trying to keep the same, will cause us stress," according to Schaef. Just like training, learning, parenting and everything in life, balance is an ongoing process. Seize it!

A TIME FOR EVERYTHING

There is a time for everything and a season for every activity under heaven: a time to be born and a time to die, a time to plant and a time to uproot, a time to kill and a time to heal, a time to tear down and a time to build, a time to weep and a time to laugh, a time to mourn and a time to dance, a time to scatter stones and a time to gather them, a time to embrace and a time to refrain, a time to search and a time to give up, a time to keep and a time to throw away, a time to tear and a time to mend, a time to be silent and a time to speak, a time to love and a time to hate, and a time for war and a time for peace. Ecclesiastics 3:1-8

We are given 168 hours a week to undertake balancing our time. While we may feel overwhelmed with trying to juggle all of our responsibilities, just remember that you are not alone and that everyone around you is also in perpetual motion trying to carry out their priorities and bring balance to their life. There is a time for everything and the key is our acceptance that we can't control it. However, we can manage it. The answer lies within our ability to discern what is important to us and then assess how much time we devote to those things we consider central to achieving balance.

SUSPEND SELECTING STRESS

Everyone seems to believe they are under enormous stress, personal and professional. Stress is blamed for many things, including overeating, smoking, drinking, unhappiness and poor marriages. If I have heard one speaker on this subject, I have heard twenty and they seemingly say the same thing. Identify your stressors and then try to eliminate or reduce them. Most people, when asked, will say they wish they had less of it in their lives. As hard as it sometimes can be to accept, stress is not something that happens to us, but rather it is something that is manufactured by our own choices. The financial stress we encounter is rarely due to something we didn't choose. No one put a gun to our head and made us apply for a credit card, drive a new car or build a bigger house. No one told us to marry young, have children, start drinking or clean our plate. Oops, that last one my mother did say. Then again, I guess I did choose how much food I put on my plate.

In order to make a difference in this lifetime, you have to stay passionate and not to allow your thinking to create stress in your life. You will never reach your potential when you are bogged down by stressful choices you make. Ultimately, it's our thinking, not our circumstances, which create much of our stress and steal our passion.

Here are some stress-management strategies that I consider to be very helpful in your selection process to suspend unnecessary stress in your life.

1. MANAGE YOUR EMOTIONS. To make a difference you have to be emotionally healthy which requires you to maintain a high degree of control over your life. When you have control of your feelings, you automatically reduce your stress.

2. PURSUE YOUR PURPOSE. People who are committed to a purpose usually view change as a challenge instead of a threat and aren't stressed in a negative way.

3. WORK YOUR PLAN. Take one thing at a time. Refrain from procrastinating. Choose how you spend your time.

4. PUT PROBLEMS INTO PERSPECTIVE. Make sure you understand the true problem and don't overestimate the importance of the problem.

5. LAUGH. When is the last time you had a good belly laugh? Take your spouse or a friend to a comedy club and have a good old fashion belly-wrenching laugh.

6. DON'T WORRY. Don't put your umbrella up until it rains. Worry restricts your ability to think and act effectively.

7. DON'T CRITICIZE YOURSELF. Our self talk and perceptions of events cause undue stress. We become what

we think, and our perception of any event will determine our reaction to it.

8. HAVE FUN. Fun is the diversion from the norm that gets us out of the rut the stressors of life can create. Go roller skating, bowling or do something you haven't done in a long time.

9. GET FRIENDLY. Give up judging, criticizing, holding grudges, unnecessary competition and the like. Earn your neighbor's love and respect. Be the person God intended you to be.

10. SEE THE GOOD. In every experience, you have to find something good. Life is about perspective. The glass is half empty or half full depending on whether you are drinking or pouring.

DOUBT YOUR DOUBTS NOT YOUR BELIEFS

As children, we envisioned performing in the adult world as some great new adventure. We weren't worried about pressure then. We only saw wondrous opportunities to prove ourselves. We closed our eyes and saw ourselves doing all kinds of amazing things. We dreamed of becoming a movie star, pro athlete or a doctor. The opportunities for us as we entered first grade were limitless. Although we may have been afraid of the newness of the situation, we were excited about so many things we were discovering. The A+ papers displayed on the refrigerator announced to the world that we were at the top of our game.

But, as we grew older and discovered our weaknesses, we started to lose confidence. We falsely assumed that not understanding algebra carries over to all aspects of ourselves. The result is that you start to see pressurized situations as opportunities to fail, rather than opportunities to succeed. You worry that sooner than later another subject will come along and be even more confusing. You don't make the lack of understanding an exception, it becomes the rule. Worse, you carry that mindset with you and, before long, you compound the pressure in your life from work and home by piling responsibility on top of responsibility. Eventually, you start seeing this as one big mess, like a mountain you couldn't possibly climb, rather than a series of actions to be taken one step at a time. Instead of accepting that algebra wasn't your strength you, with help from your parents, placed undue pressure on yourself which produced stress in other areas of your life.

You have begun to doubt yourself, and that doubt is one of the ingredients that leads to eventual failure. You have started to think of all the things you can't do rather than all the things you can do. You now see pressure as some enormous obstacle, the boulder that you must somehow push up the hill, something that is going to crush not only your performance but also your spirit. All too often it becomes a self-fulfilling prophecy. Every situation can present a new set of problems, but it can also present a new set of opportunities. You have to believe in your strengths and not allow weaknesses to overtake what you believe. Struggling with a subject in school doesn't make you a bad student. Letting it consume you and make you doubt yourself can lead to more failure. I always believed I was creative and, for as long as I can remember, was writing something for my mom to read. I actually created a family newspaper when I was in second grade. As for me and algebra – we never got along. I was positive I would in no way be a math teacher someday. As for me and creative writing – I loved it. I never stopped believing that someday I might write something someone other than my mom would read.

STAY POSITVE AND THRIVE UNDER PRESSURE

Don't let people tell you what you can't do. Only allow people to influence you when they can help you in a positive way. As I stated in an earlier chapter, spend less time and energy complaining about how much pressure you're under. This is all wasted energy, energy that could better be used for something else. Allow the changes you go through in life to make pressure an ally. At my lowest point in life, I went through overwhelming changes that could have crushed my spirits if I had succumbed to the stress. Instead, I applied the right pressure which made me stronger and brought out the best in me. I'm not sure who said it, but I have heard it a thousand times, "It's not how many times you get knocked down that matters, it's how many times you get up." Or my version, "It's not how many times you get knocked down that matters, it's how swiftly you can stop complaining about how much bigger your opponent is and figure out a way to knock them down." The day I stopped making excuses was the day I started on top.

ALLOW THE CHANGES YOU GO THROUGH IN LIFE TO MAKE PRESSURE AN ALLY.

The things we continue to excuse will return to haunt us over and over again. John Wooden was one of the greatest basketball coaches of all time. One of Wooden's memorable statements regarding people taking responsibility for their actions was, "Nobody is a real loser –

until they start blaming somebody else. Stop whining and making excuses and stay positive under pressure. There isn't good pressure and bad pressure. There is simply pressure which when approached positively will make you better and when approached negatively will make you bitter."

TAKE OFF THE BLINDERS

Once you know your purpose it gets easy, right? Wrong! As you live your life in a purposeful way and go about your daily business, many different thoughts and states of mind will surface. Regardless of your ability to let go of your past and begin to create and live your own destiny, every day you will face challenges that will thwart your ability to grow. The key to growing will be your ability to check your passion everyday and never lose it. Remember, purpose is what drives you, but it is your passion that fuels you. Knowing where you are going is the first step to making a difference. However, staying energized and passionate and continuing to grow to finish the trip is the real challenge.

THE KEY TO GROWING WILL BE YOUR ABILITY
TO CHECK YOUR PASSION EVERYDAY
AND NEVER LOSE IT.

You have to take off the blinders and add people in your life that will show you the blind spots and help you navigate through them. Your weaknesses may be their strengths. After a speech, I was asked if I had a mentor and, if I did, what was the biggest difference they made in my life? For me, that person was Margaret Shannon. She never told me what I wanted to hear. It was always what I needed to hear. Her "Margaretisms" as I like to refer to them, stuck with me all these years.

She was forever supplying me with quotes and sayings that would inspire me, as well as remind me of what was right and wrong. She knew my every weakness and loved me enough to guide me through the blind spots. Today I have a loving wife that is the co-pilot on my journey. While she may not be as blunt as Margaret, she still has a flair for keeping me on the right path. When I approach a fork in the road she always says, "Go right! You never go wrong when you go right."

So take off the blinders and, regardless of your past and all your good intentions, add some people to hold you accountable. All of your good intentions cannot fulfill that subconscious desire to be more successful. You have the right intuition, but just like a NASCAR driver, you will readily discover the value of a spotter to see the blind spots.

PASSION IS A CHOICE

Enthusiasm is an easy choice when your actions yield results, the sun is shining and everything seems to be going your way. But what about the days it's raining on your parade – when life seems to be a boring routine? Where is the enthusiasm then? It's where it always was – inside you! Passion is the pilot light on a gas fireplace, ready for you to turn the control knob to ignite it into a flame and heat the house. When it gets cold outside, that's when the knob needs to be turned up to its highest point. The same is true for the times in your life when things seem to be the bleakest or most despondent. That's the time to be the most passionate! For me, passion is about the "why." Why you do what you do provides the motivation for doing it. I always tell people that I never focus on the travel part of my job. If I did, I would never speak again. My fuel (passion) is reminding myself about the people I can possibly influence. I can't change people, but the thought of saying something that motivates them to change lights a huge fire in my heart and soul. So many times we focus on our individual responsibly and fail to connect the dots on how what we do can impact so many other people with our daily lives. Family, friends, neighbors, co-workers and everyone you come in contact with provide your opportunities to make a difference.

WHY YOU DO WHAT YOU DO PROVIDES THE MOTIVATION FOR DOING IT.

When faced with a routine chore such as typing a letter, filing papers, filling out forms, cutting the grass or just cleaning up, approach each task as if it were the first time you faced it. I am passionate about cutting the grass. I am! When I prepare to cut the grass, I guard against making it anything but routine. From the music blaring in the garage to the cooler of beverages chilling in the shade, I make cutting the grass anything but typical. Each time I speak to an audience, I envision their smiles, their nods of affirmation and the great feedback I always receive when I am finished. It is always the first time for me. Although it may be the two thousandth time to present a keynote speech, it is always the first time for that audience. When my former secretary Margaret first asked me the question, "Why did the chicken cross the road?" I was humored by her response to my answer. I said, "It crosses the road to get to the other side," to which she said, "You have become the chicken! You just cross the road everyday to get to the other side without any regard to experience, exploration or discovery. Instead of crossing the road like it is the first time, you just do it routinely which takes all of the enthusiasm and passion out of it." Wow! It's like when we were children and visited a place for the very first time. The excitement of discovery is contagious. When my wife and I travel to an unfamiliar

80

city, we enter the situation generally with the attitude of what can we see that's new. What will surprise us? It may be the thousandth sales call, hundredth piano lesson or fiftieth time you've done something. Expect it to be different from every one that preceded it. It may be the four thousandth time I have kissed my wife, but it is always like the first when I approach it with love, enthusiasm and passion.

DRINK FROM THE GARDEN HOSE

We all too often focus our attention on what happiness isn't rather than on what it is. As I sit in my hotel room, I can't help but notice the bottle of water to the right of me that has a small sign on it that says, "Enjoy a delicious bottle of fresh spring water for only $5." Is it me or have we completely lost our common sense? We will pay $15 for the equivalent of 64 ounces of water in a bottle and yet stress out over the price of a gallon (64 ounces) of gas when it reaches $3. We have made it all so convoluted. Do you remember playing outside on a hot summer day before the technological revolution drove children indoors? This was back in the days when your neighborhood was your playground, not your computer. Can you also recollect when you were playing outside and got thirsty? You found the closest garden hose, turned it on, let the rust and warm water rush through it, and when it became cold enough to drink, you guzzled it like soda. You were happy to have a cold sip of water and weren't focused on where it was coming from. Happiness is that break that rejuvenates our spirit that comes from within. It consists of not having, but of being. The basis of happiness is to love something outside of self. Most of us have many brief moments of happiness every day, regardless of what else is going on. The key is to notice them!

STOP KIDDING YOURSELF

We get so busy and so involved with the rush of living, we not only miss opportunities, we all too often spend our most productive years in the pursuit of things that are not really important. If you honestly stand back and get some perspective on this situation, it seems quite foolish. Yet, we live in a society that will rationalize every unimportant activity we are investing our time and energy into and make it legitimate. There are five things that you cannot recover in life: The stone after it's thrown, the word after it's said, the occasion after it's missed, the time after it's gone and a person after they die. You don't get a practice life. You must seize the opportunities now!

Social media, whether Twitter, Facebook or LinkedIn, are changing the way we live. Indeed, we might feel as if we are suddenly awash in friends. However, upon further examination, it is changing the way we conduct relationships. With the relationship pattern changing, our capacity to make a difference in people's lives is becoming more restricted. Friends sit with one another across the course of their lives, savoring its moments, bitter and sweet. The era has arrived where electronic stimuli have replaced the joys of human contact. We have misled ourselves to believe that the numerous Facebook acquaintances, which sometimes number in the hundreds, somehow keeps us more connected than the small circle of friends we once had. Connected to what? Just as our daily lives are becoming more technologically connected, we're losing other more meaningful relationships. We may be connected, but we are losing our friends. According to Aristotle and the ancient Greeks, you can have everything that life can offer – career, family and money, but if a person doesn't have a good friend, his or her life is fundamentally lacking.

WE HAVE REACHED AN ERA WHERE ELECTRONIC STIMULI HAVE REPLACED THE JOYS OF HUMAN CONTACT.

We learn how to make friends, or not, in our most formative years, as children. School, homework (with a little resistance and a few distractions), organized extracurricular activities, family time and play time with friends and neighbors used to be the norm. The new millennium ushered in a new list – school, homework (with a lot of resistance and numerous distractions), few extracurricular activities, limited family time and electronic devices which have replaced play time or time just to "hang out." If there is a secret to close friendship, that's it. Put down the device. Engage the person. According to a study published in the *American Sociological Review*, the average American has only two close friends and a quarter don't have any. A connection may be a click away, but cultivating a good friendship takes more. "Social connectivity" is not the same as intimate friendship. While social networking has grown exponentially, the quality of the connections is shallow. Advances in technology have networked us as never before, and we continue to connect with friends and family via e-mail and text messages. Unfortunately, face-to-face moments are fleeting and, in a high percentage of cases, they are rescheduled and interrupted dozens of times.

REDUCE THE E-STRACTIONS

Despite our numerous technological and scientific advances, we are nurturing a culture of detachment. We have managed to take the inconsequential and make it important by making it more immediate.

Remember when Stephen Covey challenged us not to let the urgent get in the way of the important? Now our greatest challenge is not to let the trivial, which is now immediate, get in the way of the important. In the workplace, the various technological distractions are deteriorating the level at which an employee can perform. At school, texting is undermining the teacher's ability to teach and the student's ability to learn. At home, we are losing opportunities to build deeper relationships with our families because we are plugged into our own bedroom-based media centers.

WE HAVE MANAGED TO TAKE THE INCONSEQUENTIAL AND MAKE IT IMPORTANT BY MAKING IT MORE IMMEDIATE.

In this ever-changing world, we are facing more and more distractions that obstruct us from truly enjoying the ride. Our hyper-mobile, cyber-centric and interruption-driven lives erode our capacity for sustained focus and awareness. They have impeded our ability to connect, reflect and relax (the secrets to coping with a mobile, multitasking, virtual world). From the classroom to corporate offices, children and adults are losing their ability to be attentive. Unfortunately, without the powers of focus, awareness and judgment, we are incapable of fending off distractions, setting goals and managing the complexity of our responsibilities.

One of the great ironies of the high-tech revolution is that devices meant to facilitate communication are actually helping to destroy it. The "anxiety of connection" has surfaced from the expectation that you will respond immediately to a message. These distractions wear down your ability to stay focused on your priorities and stay attentive to the task at hand. Although attention is not always within our control, we nevertheless rationalize why our children have cell phones and why we check our email at all hours of the day and night. The greatest menace to connecting with our children is purchasing them a cell phone, but the illusion is that it keeps you connected. Because we virtually check in with one another all day, the act of moving across a physical threshold becomes devoid of meaning. The conversations that used to take place at the dinner table between families in homes all across America have been slowly replaced by text messages. Only 17% of the families in a recent UCLA study consistently ate dinner together.

GET A TUNE UP

Most people take better care of their cars than they do themselves. If you are ever going to seize the opportunities, you have to be in the right frame of mind to take hold of them. Opportunities always look bigger going than coming, so it is essential that you take the time to prepare for their arrival so you don't miss them. Next time you go for an oil change and have the tires rotated, remind yourself that you too need a tune-up.

✓ RELAX – it is what it is

✓ RENEW – replenish yourself and do something fun

✓ REALIZE – appreciate what you have

✓ RECOGNIZE – your limits

✓ REVIVE – the passion you once had for something

STOP JUSTIFYING THE UNIMPORTANT

In a world of speed and overload, it is crucial that you take a step back and remind yourself what is important. People have become chess pieces in a world that is void of human interaction and connectivity. With self-serve airport kiosks, ATM's, online grocery delivery service, clothing catalogs, restaurant reservations and the ability to order a pizza for delivery online, it has become possible to bypass almost every possible human interaction. Every day a passenger on an airplane thinks their selfish need is more important than safety. Imagine what you would think if the pilot of the plane was reacting to a text message from his son or daughter while trying to take off or land? However, we still have a choice! Even though we are living in an e-driven culture that interrupts our family time, distracts us at work and eradicates the need for personal contact, ultimately the choice still remains with us. Cell phones, home computers, blackberries and iPods are still luxuries and not necessities. The evolution of the cell phone is evidence of this statement. When you had to pay roaming charges on every call you made, you didn't see the need to make as many calls. When you had to purchase a phone at regular retail price and the price to add another number was expensive, your children somehow didn't need a phone. When there was a substantial charge to send and receive text messages, you were able to live without them. This affordability and ease has allowed us to rationalize how we use our cell phones and why everyone in the family has one. We manufacture every possible reason to defend our use of cell phones, blackberries and computers and in some cases, even go against school rules and company policies. Video games, TV and computers have replaced imaginative and outside play and problem solving through play. Imaginative play creates neural pathways that instant gratification technology can't do. This is a wake-up call to balance the wonderful world of technology with activities that also enhance creativity. Adults can take breaks from technology to shut off the noise in the brain, but children won't do that without encouragement. If we don't help them make those decisions, we are helping create a world of young people who are increasingly disconnected from the physical world.

EVEN THOUGH WE ARE LIVING IN AN E-DRIVEN
CULTURE THAT INTERRUPTS OUR FAMILY TIME,
DISTRACTS US AT WORK AND ERADICATES THE
NEED FOR PERSONAL CONTACT, ULTIMATELY
THE CHOICE STILL REMAINS WITH US.

It's time to cut the e-leash and reduce or eliminate as many e-stractions in your personal and professional life as you possibly can. As we depart this earth, we will leave everything behind except the influence and impression we have made on others. The quality of our work, the eminence of our family and the significance of our friendships will ultimately be determined by our capacity to keep centered on what is truly important. It is time to eliminate the e-stractions and re-connect, reflect and seize the opportunities.

BROADEN YOUR PERSPECTIVE

A buzz phrase of the late 80's was "think big picture." A long-range outlook is one of the most valuable gifts we can have. Some believe that perspective can only come with age and experience. Both help, however, anyone can have perspective or not have it. Perspective is gained by rising above the day-to-day and seeing a bigger representation of the circumstances while still contributing to what is going on at the moment. The opportunities that take in life's tests are sometimes never realized because although we have access to knowledge we never seek it out. There is nothing wrong with not having a greater perspective. However, when you have an option to gain one, you are foolish not to. We deprive ourselves of possible growth when we do not reward ourselves with the viewpoints around us. Maybe what is worse, yet, is having a perspective and listening to another person's outlook with no intention of even considering it. Why even ask for it? Instead of learning, growing and expanding our vision from a different perspective, we turn a deaf ear to the ideas and stay the course with our own narrow-minded view. When people tell me the glass is either half full or half empty, I remind them that it is all dependent on whether you are pouring or drinking.

EXPAND YOUR WORLD

Many people get into the habit of saying no to new experiences, preferring to be locked into a comfort zone that restricts their growth. For example, my mother with all her great qualities, tends to approach life with security and familiarity. Her life has become habitual rather than pragmatic. Existing in a world ruled by habit can lead to routine and schedules. Stop proclaiming, "Just wait until you get to be my age." Life is a smorgasbord, a variety of tasty, delicious choices that have nothing to do with age and everything to do with opportunity. People locked into a comfort zone pass over any opportunities that may be foreign to them. Their selection is based on familiarity. What you become is far more important than what you are. Why? Because this is the only way life gets better. One of the three keys to success is growing to reach your potential, which requires you to take an inventory regarding who you are and, more importantly, what you can become. You must develop an appetite for the unique and unusual.

Your ideas, thoughts, information, activities and insights are the means to seize the opportunities which may pass you by if you don't expand who you are. Growth comes from the inside, not the outside, and unless we enlarge ourselves, we'll always have what we've got. No more, no less. For some, that is how they define contentment. Fair enough, but contentment is no replacement for what you are capable of and what you are intended to be.

YOUR IDEAS, THOUGHTS, INFORMATION, ACTIVITIES AND INSIGHTS ARE THE MEANS TO SEIZE THE OPPORTUNITIES WHICH MAY PASS YOU BY IF YOU DON'T EXPAND WHO YOU ARE.

I am reminded of a woman who applied for a creative position at our company that would have meant a promotion for her. She submitted her application, but someone who had been with our company far less time than she was hired instead. Outraged, she went to our human resource manager and asked why. The director of human resources said, "I'm sorry, but you haven't had 22 years of experience as your application states. You've had only one year's experience 22 times. This unfortunate situation occurs far too often. This woman never improved or grew beyond her initial value to our company. You have to become expandable or you, too often, become expendable. Don't feel trapped or inadequate. Stop admiring everyone else's good fortune and seize the opportunities in front of you.

OUTGROW YOUR POSITION

It seems like yesterday that I was in Overland Park, Kansas, auditioning for a seminar company who was in quest of speakers who could present their seminars all across the country. Fresh off of a great eleven-year career at a greeting card company, where I served at three different levels of leadership, I was primed for my new opportunity. At the tryout, every speaker was hearing the same thing, and all I could think about was, "Am I capable of becoming a successful speaker?" Before I knew it, one of the leaders in the company announced that we were already halfway to being successful professional speakers. His exact words were, "Success is deciding what you like to do and then determining how to be successful doing it." Great advice and, although not necessarily easy, it was at that moment I harnessed my passion and determined to be relentless in my pursuit of every possibility surrounding speaking.

SUCCESS IS DECIDING WHAT YOU LIKE TO DO AND THEN DETERMINING HOW TO BE SUCCESSFUL DOING IT.

Following my eight-minute audition in front of a speech coach, company vice president and several other people from the company, I was approached by the person in charge of booking speakers who said, "Your goal needs to be to outgrow our company." A bit confused, I responded with a morsel of naivety and said, "Does this mean you plan to subcontract with me to speak at your seminars?" With a big smile, she responded, "Absolutely! Of all the speakers we previewed today, you have the most potential to outgrow our company and go on to speak on a much larger stage. As a matter of fact, I believe that we will simply be a stepping stone for you to smooth out the edges and take away the insecurities you may now have as a speaker. I firmly believe you will outgrow us if you work hard enough, and your only challenge then will be not to become a prima donna."

DON'T FEAR DIFFERENCES

Succumbing to the fear of differences is a very good way to stay stagnant and miss too many opportunities. When we have to deal with someone very different from ourselves, we tend to retreat to distance ourselves. Company boards are a proliferation of this principle. People who serve on boards tend to see differences and immediately pull back into themselves. They surreptitiously establish who and what they are and their way of doing things and then judge the other person for being different. How do I know? Been there, done that, got the hat, t-shirt, key chain and bumper sticker.

What are we afraid of? Why do we have to remake everyone else in our own image to feel comfortable with them? After all, aren't the best teams made up of diverse people who bring different talents, ideas and opinions to the table? Our natural tendency in new and unknown situations is to try to reach into our "what we know" and define the situation from that point of view. When I turned the corner in my business is when I let my employees challenge my assumptions. More than once a young kid, officially known as my son, was exactly what I needed. When I begin to embrace my differences, it opened up more possibilities and created an edge for us. Today, with two sons, a daughter-in-law and wife as part of that corporate team, I am a better speaker, author and business person.

UNCERTAINTY IS A PART OF LIFE

One thing is for certain – life is filled with uncertainty. It is impossible to know what the next 24 hours or, for that matter, the next hour will bring. Blessings and sorrows, success and failure, sunshine and rain are all present in life's agenda. The fear of uncertainty can have a crippling effect on our pursuit of making a difference.

In the Middle Ages, European sailors refused to sail very far south. They were convinced that the middle of the earth was ringed with fire, because the farther south they traveled the hotter the temperature became. The fear of the unknown kept the Atlantic Ocean free from explorers. Sometime in the Middle Ages, a chart was drawn showing a painting of a ship turning back in the Mediterranean Sea from the Strait of Gibraltar. Above the painting appears the Latin phrase, *Ne Plus Ultra*, which means "Nothing more beyond." Had it not been for Ponce de Leon and Christopher Columbus, the Atlantic Ocean would have remained an undiscovered horizon. They challenged the myths of what might lie beyond to discover new worlds and unexplored possibilities.

How many of life's horizons go unexplored because we fear the uncertainties or are satisfied to tiptoe through life to make it safely to death without seeing what is available to us? The road to disappointment, in fact, is besieged with plentiful overlooked opportunities. Countless discoveries await the adventurous spirit willing to test the unknown, seize the opportunities and make an enormous difference.

CHAPTER AFTERTHOUGHT

Consider...

❖ Taking a 10-30 minute walk every day. While you walk, smile. It is the ultimate antidepressant.

❖ Playing more games and reading more books.

❖ Spending time with people over the age of 70 and under the age of 6.

❖ Doing more when you are awake.

❖ Trying to make at least three people smile each day.

❖ Not wasting your precious energy on gossip or issues of the past, negative thoughts or things you cannot control. Instead, invest your energy in the positive, present moment.

❖ Life isn't fair, but it's all good.

❖ Life is too short to hate anyone.

❖ Not taking yourself so seriously.

❖ Not having to win every argument. Be happy, not right.

❖ Making peace with your past so it won't spoil the present.

❖ Not comparing your life to others. You have no idea what their journey is about.

❖ Taking charge of your happiness.

❖ Forgiving everyone for everything.

❖ Realizing what other people think of you is none of your business.

❖ God heals everything!

❖ However good or bad a situation is, it will change.

❖ Reminding yourself that no matter how you feel, get up, dress up and show up.

❖ Doing the right thing.

❖ Remembering that you are too blessed to be stressed.

❖ That you only have one ride through life, so make the most of it and *Enjoy The Ride*™.

4

MAXIMIZE YOUR POTENTIAL

Generate and maintain

a burning desire for

your purpose.

MAXIMIZE YOUR POTENTIAL

P eople who make a difference and perform at a high level all have something in common – traits and attributes that make them successful. The first trait of difference makers is belief in their dreams. As you learned in Chapter 2, you have to dream big. Performance is not a measure of value – it's a reflection of it. You perform up to the expectation that you and significant others have for you in advance. So the expectation equals motivation. Motivation is an inner force that compels behavior. The most important belief you will ever have concerns your potential. Why would you be motivated to learn if you didn't think you were worth the effort? You must look at yourself as an uncut gem of potential – a diamond in the rough that only needs to be cut and polished with experience, skills and knowledge.

THE MOST IMPORTANT OPINION YOU WILL EVER HAVE IS THE ONE IN YOUR HEAD.

Belief is the single most important thing. I believe I can do something more than I am doing, and I won't let anything stop me. You project on the outside what you feel on the inside. The most important opinion you will ever have is the one in your head. With belief in yourself, you can cultivate your talents and make a difference.

Talent is inborn. You will never have another ounce of talent because it was given to you at the moment you were conceived. It's a combination of all the marvelous things that came before you. For example, the ability to sit in front of a piano and play it without a lesson is a talent that is inborn. My stepson, Adam, has an infatuation with music and he possesses a talent, that when pursued and uncovered, can bud and blossom. The things you love to do in the evenings and on weekends show where your talents lie. When you begin to believe in your talents and your worth, you ignite an emotion that fuels a desire and takes you to another level. Anne Wilson Schaef believes self-acceptance, self-exploration, self-improvement, self-reliance, self-understanding and self-centeredness are vital to living in balance. Balance is essential to maximizing your potential.

SELF-ACCEPTANCE

"What person other than ourselves can we be sure will be with us from the moment of conception until the last breath leaves our body? We may look for a love to be with us always and even the love of our life will not have the same duration with ourselves that we do. Let's face it: If we are looking for longevity in our relationships, we're it! Now that we have established the point of longevity, let's explore some of the factors that may limit our romance with ourselves. This is the easiest love affair of our lives and we don't want to miss it.

WHEN WE ADMIT OUR MISTAKES AND MAKE
AMENDS FOR THEM, WE RECLAIM OUR POWER
AND ACTUALLY LIKE OURSELVES BETTER.

SELF-RELIANCE

"Self-reliance is part of the bend of the American culture. It is a principle that supplies much of how and what we think and feel. Yet, self-reliance is a difficult issue for many of us. Self-reliance has been twisted to mean that we have to do everything for ourselves, that asking for help is an act of losing face. In our culture, heroes are people who really never need anyone else (and even when they accept help they don't really need it).

A former employee of mine always felt like she failed when she didn't know how to do everything herself. She would go beyond her comfort level of expertise and not only stress herself out, but make a simple challenge a full blown calamity. This self-reliant philosophy that guided her also confined her. Her beliefs, illusions, and philosophies about doing everything herself were the beginning of the end. She tried to be so self-sufficient that she didn't know how to function cooperatively. With time she became defensive, protective and territorial. William Ernest Hocking said, "We cannot climb up a rope that is attached only to our own belt." Regrettably, in the end she "gave up" because she unconsciously held on to a belief in self-reliance but she just couldn't do it all. Like the dieter who hides food throughout the house, this employee covered up work which she couldn't accomplish. The unfortunate thing was that because of her lack of self-acceptance, her self-reliance was the mechanism she used to overcompensate and be who we thought she should be instead of who she really was.

In this lifetime, each of us is invited to learn, take responsibility, and use our talents. Nonetheless, may I also remind you that a rope held by many hands is stronger than a rope only held by one."

SELF-UNDERSTANDING

"So many brilliant and gifted people, who could make a huge difference in their lifetime, squander their gifts because they lack the humility of self-understanding. When we think we know it all, we miss the point. The greatest journey we will ever take is the journey into ourselves, for we are all microcosms of all that is. We can learn, and need to learn, from all that is around us. The mastery of life is the mastery of self. Self-understanding rarely comes from thinking or analyzing ourselves. Self-understanding is soul awareness. It comes with allowing that knowledge that is within us to emerge. When we think we know everything about ourselves, we show our ignorance and our arrogance. The wonder of human beings is that we are constructed in such a way that we can spend our entire lives exploring our inner self and still barely scratch the surface. Never stop learning about yourself because self-understanding is a process that is never complete.

WHEN WE THINK WE KNOW IT ALL, WE MISS THE POINT.

When you truly step back and learn more about who you are your potential for growth increases. The greatest example is when two people split-up and end their relationship, and one says, "I just need more time to find out who I really am." The actuality is that they really do; however, the reality is they rarely do. We fool ourselves into believing we have enough. Growing to reach your potential requires tenacity for knowledge. We are a wonder for us to behold!"

SELF-CENTEREDNESS

"Just because we don't know how to do something and have not found a way to work it out, we come to the conclusion that it doesn't exist. Self-centeredness is so limiting and so destructive. Self-centeredness is not taking care of oneself as some believe. It is the process of being out of touch with oneself while focusing completely on the "I." The state of self-centeredness is so powerful that it expands to fill in whatever space is there. People who live around self-centeredness often become self-centered themselves because they reach a state where they begin to feel that they have to grab something for themselves. Self-centeredness is contagious! The worst thing about self-centeredness is that when we are immersed in it, we don't know it, and we haven't a clue how to get out of it.

WHEN WE ARE SELF-CENTERED, DOWN DEEP
WE BELIEVE THAT IF WE DID NOT CREATE IT, OR
MAKE IT HAPPEN, IT SIMPLY DOES NOT EXIST.

How asinine can self-centeredness be? We are so busy wanting people to love us, believing we can control who will love us, when, in what way, and under what conditions, being afraid that people will love us, resulting in a huge list of demands that we do not want to meet, being so sure that we really deep down are not lovable and that when people get to know us they will walk away, that we don't have time to stop and see that we have people in our lives who really do love us. When we are self-centered, down deep we believe that if we did not create it, or make it happen, it simply does not exist. We are so busy trying to get our needs met that we fail to see the possibility of more abundance than we could imagine all around us. We can't see the world around us because we spend so much time being in our own way. We become so absorbed in trying to manipulate people and circumstances to get what we need that we would not be able to see what we really need if it hit us over the head. One cannot get out of self-centeredness through self-will. The way to deal with self-centeredness is to do things for others, to be of service. Self-centeredness is harming to us and to others. It is not worth what it costs us."

MAKE THE MOST OF YOUR SECOND CHANCES

I believe in second chances! As Helen Prejean said, "People are more than the worst thing they have ever done in their lives." There is a tendency to believe that people who have done something wrong or bad are bad people and will always be bad people. There is a deep, usually hidden and unspoken belief that people can't really change and that they are no more than "the worst thing they have ever done in their lives." This belief results in a great deal of secret keeping and the need to try to keep our pasts hidden. When I met my wife, Diane, the first thing she said was, "We both have a past and that is exactly what it is, the past."

I believe people can learn and grow from their mistakes if they can forgive themselves. Once that occurs, then the greatest opportunities for learning and growing are waiting to be discovered. For me personally, the worst thing I ever did was the most important because it offered me the opportunity to learn and practice the process of forgiveness. I also learned that self-forgiveness is conceivably the most difficult of all. Second chances are only advantageous if we acknowledge our mistake, learn the lessons from it, forgive ourselves and move on. For me, that took more than a few weeks or months. By the time I finished beating myself up, all of the critics were standing in line to throw the first stone. People who didn't even know all the facts were making heavily-weighted negative judgments. My best friend, Todd, always reminded me that without the knowledge of the facts and outlook of concern, an opinion is simply that – an opinion! As Margaret once said, "It requires less mental effort to condemn than to think."

THE PROCESS OF FORGIVENESS IS ONE OF THE MOST IMPORTANT PROCESSES WE CAN LEARN IN LIFE, AND SELF-FORGIVENESS IS PERHAPS THE MOST DIFFICULT OF ALL.

Second chances allow us to approach each day as a new day which, of course, it is. There is something about the freshness in the idea of a new day that encourages us to forgive ourselves from past mistakes and give life a new try. I know firsthand that when you get a second chance, it brings you the opportunity to come up with fresh ideas, fresh approaches and fresh behaviors. It allows you to approach each morning as a new day with new possibilities. I became a better son, husband, father and friend. Embrace your second chances and see what happens. The only thing you have to lose is all the guilt which can hold you back from ever reaching our potential.

DON'T COUNT YOUR CHICKENS BEFORE THEY HATCH

Most people have a tendency to count their chickens before they hatch. It's a tendency we must work hard to overcome as we move to maximize our potential. Success isn't handed to anyone on a silver platter. No one has a sure lock on happiness, a great career or lots of money. Time and talents are given to us. So is the ability to imagine and envision the future. Do you deserve success? Absolutely! You owe it to yourself to achieve through maximizing your potential. Do other people have an obligation to make you successful? Absolutely not! Are you looking to someone else today to enable you to live the dream life you want to live? Are you expecting someone else to pave your road to success while you sit back and squander your potential? Face the facts. Your potential and ultimate success is your responsibility, not that of anyone else. Be cautious if the victory seems too easy. It isn't that you shouldn't rejoice in your win. It's that success is not a constant. It is always a transition. Former Super Bowl winning coach, Dick Vermeil, believes, "You shouldn't judge your potential or ultimate success or failure by the first win or loss." Ultimately, you will never arrive at the absolute of your potential. Potential is a concept akin to growth. You never fully grow up, no matter how old you become in years. There is always more maturity, more growth, more development, more refinement and more achievement possible.

"YOU SHOULDN'T JUDGE YOUR POTENTIAL OR
ULTIMATE SUCCESS OR FAILURE
BY THE FIRST WIN OR LOSS."

Whenever you reach the point where you say to yourself, "I have it made, I've got all the success I can possibly have, I have reached my potential," be wary. You are on the verge of overconfidence and overconfidence can lead to pride and carelessness. That can lead to a disastrous fall. As my mother has said a thousand times, "Pride goes before the fall." When you reach a point of believing you are invincible, you're on the verge of some major disappointment. Carelessness and reckless moves are made when new plans aren't. Irritability erupts when new problems arise. Anxiety attacks occur when fear of failure rears its ugly head. I constantly remind myself, my family and the people within our business that success isn't permanent, so don't expect it to be.

DON'T COMPARE YOURSELF TO OTHERS

Comparison rarely benefits anyone. I am constantly meeting people who are smarter, younger, older, wiser, richer, more creative and working just as hard or harder than I am. Anytime I have made comparisons, I seemingly have ended up being discouraged. This is a detriment to my growth. I can always find other speakers who don't measure up to what I have become or am aspiring to be. I have disciplined myself and avoided the tendency to compare myself to them. If I don't, I'll lower my expectations and settle for less than what I am capable of. In the professional speaking industry, comparison is a common occurrence. Some speakers come to think they deserve more success than others or that success lies ahead for them, no matter what they do. Both are false assumptions. In truth, potential isn't a pie with a limited number of pieces. The potential of others has very little bearing on your potential. Neither is your potential maximized by what others say or accomplish. Only you can truly define what you are capable of, and only you can measure it. As we endeavor to reach our potential, we must resist the temptation to see how others are doing and keep track of whether they are behind us, passing us or pulling away from us. The only thing that truly counts is how we live our own life and whether we have the endurance to maximize our God-given talents.

STOP PRETENDING

If you are ever going to take full advantage of your potential and light the passionate fires within yourself, then live your life without pretense. Just going to church doesn't make you a Christian any more than standing in a garage makes you a mechanic. Every saint has a past and every sinner has a future. When we are pretending to be something or someone we are not, we cannot help but feel uneasy. We are always looking over our shoulders lest we be found out. Sometimes we fear that if we become too good at pretending, we will be fooled and will forget who we really are. Then there is always the uneasiness of not knowing if our friends like us because of who they think we are or because of who we really are. The longer we pretend, the more difficult it is for us to break the pattern.

WHEN WE ARE PRETENDING TO BE SOMETHING
OR SOMEONE WE ARE NOT, WE CANNOT
HELP BUT FEEL UNEASY.

Why do we have such a problem with the simplicity of just being who we are? We may be "unusual," slightly odd or even very creative. The important issue is that we are perfectly unique. There never has been and never will be anyone like us. We are a one-time creation and can add much more to the world when we are just ourselves. The world needs our unique contributions. You were born an original, so don't die a copy or, worse yet, something you are not. We can imagine to be someone else and even dupe a small number of people, but at the conclusion of our life, who we, in fact, are will be uncovered. The following poem offers some perspective.

I was shocked, confused, and bewildered as I entered heaven's door. Not by the beauty of it all, nor the lights or its décor; but it were folks in Heaven who made me sputter and gasp. There stood the kid from seventh grade who swiped my lunch money twice. Next to him was my old neighbor who never said anything nice. I nudged Jesus and said, "What's the deal?" How did all these sinners get up here? And why is everyone so quiet and so somber? "Hush child," he said, "They are all in shock. No one thought they would be seeing you."

TURN KNOWLEDGE INTO POWER

To reach your potential, you must become well-rounded by developing knowledge. Start by writing down one skill you will start focusing on, developing or improving. Then write down one failure you had in your life and three things learned from it. In my book, *Mum's The Word*, I share that the lessons that are learned are the wisdom that is earned. The failures we experience can serve as a launch pad to make us stronger and wiser. They also sometimes serve in helping us raise the bar.

SOMETIMES THE THINGS WE ARE MOST
PASSIONATE ABOUT ESCAPE US NOT
BECAUSE OF A LACK OF TALENT, BUT RATHER
BECAUSE WE LACK THE RESOLVE NECESSARY
TO PURSUE THEM.

From time to time, we can become even more than we believe we were capable of because our failures force us into directions where we would have never ventured because of doubt and fear. From my senior year in high school when I emceed our senior banquet, I was always passionate about speaking. People always commented on how I had been given a talent to perform in front of people and do it in a humorous and entertaining way. Sometimes the things we are most passionate about escape us not because of a lack of talent, but rather because we lack the resolve necessary to pursue them. You must look at yourself as an uncut gem of potential. You must believe in your passion and invest the time and energy in developing the skills and training regime of a champion. You have to go full speed ahead and work hard at being successful.

LEARN SOMETHING NEW

Professors have a long-established practice of taking time off. Every seven years, fully tenured professors are, by tradition, granted a semester or an entire year to replenish themselves professionally and intellectually. Most dedicate this time to a particular task, a trip abroad to conduct on-site research to pursue original source material or a series of guest lectures at another location. The experiences are thought-provoking and the timing is intense.

You can do the same for yourself. Take a break to learn something new. Explore a new interest. Acquire a new proficiency. Don't allow it to derail you from your goals or purposes. Rather, seek what will complement your goals and enrich you personally. Taking time out periodically to renew yourself helps you maintain the self-confidence that you need to maximize your potential and make a difference.

SWEAT THE SMALL STUFF

The *small* stuff makes a *big* difference!

I will forever remember the day I went to meet the president of Adecco at their corporate offices in Charlotte, North Carolina. As I approached the elevator in the parking garage adjacent to their building, I noticed a sign on the wall by the elevator that said, "Don't forget where you parked...Take One!" On a business-size card it stated, Charlotte Plaza Parking Garage, Welcome, You Have Parked Your Car On Level 4. I took a card, smiled and entered the elevator thinking what a difference something that little makes.

I always appreciate the hotels who remind us of the choice we can make to impact our children's children. At the Woodlands Resort and Conference Center, they have a card on your bed that states, "Place this card on the bed in the morning if you would like to have a fresh set of linens. Please leave towels to be washed on the floor or hang towels you wish to reuse on the rack. YOUR CHOICE MAKES A DIFFER-ENCE. Together we can reduce chlorine and detergent use and save millions of gallons of water." Again, a small matter to some, but a huge difference maker to many.

What would a book about making a difference be if we didn't mention the fact that all Starbucks employees, full time and part time, receive stock options and healthcare coverage? Treat people like family and they will be loyal and give you their all. It's an old formula in business that is second nature to many family-run firms, but since the 1980's it seems to have been forgotten. I remember the first year my daughter-in-law worked for us and she received a Thanksgiving card with a $50 gift card enclosed to purchase a turkey or ham. Her response was simply, "That's why people are so loyal to you."

THE FRIENDLY SKIES

Allow me to introduce a person who not only sweats the small stuff, but is a living example of someone who maximizes his potential. Denny Flanagan is a captain for United Airlines and an incredible one at that. Since his childhood, he always desired to be a pilot. Now that he is a pilot, he truly makes a difference every day. While he is on the aircraft for your safety, he also does numerous things that make you rapidly realize he is a difference maker. His crew briefs are not typical. He places his hand over his heart and thanks the flight attendants and first officer for the great job they do. He reminds them of the impact they have on the customer and that because of their service, customers purchase another ticket. If there are any unaccompanied children between the ages of 5 and 14 on the flight, he always requests the information packet so he can call their mother and let her know what seat her child has and that the flight attendants are taking good care of them. He wants to let the crew know he cares.

Before each flight, Denny goes out into the boarding area to greet the customers. He speaks into the microphone at the gate and lets them know he is the captain of the flight they are taking, informs them the plane is in great shape and that this is his first flight. He gives more details about the flight and ensures that every person flying that day knows how much he cares. On numerous occasions, his pre-flight greeting is met with laughter and applause. As you board the aircraft, he greets you and thanks you for your business while handing you a trading card that has all the facts about the plane you are boarding.

Two big difference makers concern strollers and pets. Denny makes sure that any family who gate checks a stroller has it the moment they walk off the plane. He or his 1st officer, makes the trip outside after landing to retrieve the stroller. People bring their pets and are anxious to know if they have been boarded. During the preflight when he walks around the aircraft to check its condition for flight, he will take a photo of the animal with his phone camera. He then gives the phone to the flight attendant so she can go back in the cabin and show the family that their pet is safe and on board. One of Denny's colleagues, Captain Pam Rae even goes so far as to offer to walk the dog beneath the plane.

So why does Denny go so far to make a difference? Statistics reveal that only ten percent of the customers traveling want to be there. Denny believes that each customer deserves a good travel experience, regardless of the airline they choose. Maybe one of the greatest examples of how he makes a difference is when any of his flights experience a weather or mechanical delay. He, not the gate agent, makes the announcement to the passengers. Part of his announcement is that he will be back in a few minutes to walk among the customers and answer any questions they may have. After the announcement he boards the aircraft and asks the flight attendants to make a pot of coffee. He explains the plan to serve coffee to the customers in the boarding area. The flight attendants always supply him with the essentials – serving tray, cups, cream, sugar and stir sticks. In most cases, they are more than happy to assist. What difference does this make? A complete transformation – the frowns turn into smiles. How much time did it take to make a difference? Not much! When you think about it – what else would Denny be doing during the delay?

So the next time you hear the United Airlines advertisement about the "friendly skies", remember that a pilot by the name of Denny Flanagan lives their advertisement. Not only is he a great person, and someone who will make your heart smile, he truly makes a difference every day of his life. He maximizes his potential every day, in every situation.

CHAPTER AFTERTHOUGHT

The people that make a difference in your life...

1. Name the last five winners of the Miss America pageant.

2. Name ten people who have won the Nobel or Pulitzer Prize.

3. Name the last half dozen Academy Award winners for best actor.

4. Name the last five Super Bowl winners in the NFL.

5. Name the last five World Series champions in MLB.

How did you do? The point is, none of us remembers the headliners of yesterday. None of these are second-rate achievers and they are the best in their fields. But the applause dies, the awards tarnish, achievements are forgotten and the accolades and certificates are buried with their owners. Here are a few more questions. See how well you do with these.

1. List a teacher who aided your journey through school.

2. Name two friends who have helped you through a difficult time.

3. Name five people who have taught you something worthwhile.

4. Think of a few people who have made you feel appreciated and special.

5. Think of five people who you enjoy spending time with.

I am sure you found it was a lot easier answering these five questions. The lesson is very simple. The people who make the biggest difference in your life are not the ones with the most credentials, the most money or the most awards – they are simply the ones who care the most.

5

DISCOVER
TRUE WEALTH

You have not lived a perfect day, even

though you have earned your money,

unless you have done something for someone

who will never be able to repay you.

DISCOVER
TRUE WEALTH

D r. Charles Dickson tells of a man who stopped at a flower shop to have flowers wired to his mother 200 miles away. As he left, he noticed a little girl sobbing on the curb in front of the shop. When he inquired what was wrong, she explained that she wanted to buy a rose for her mother, but it cost $2.00 and she only had 75 cents. He bought the rose for the girl and offered her a ride home. She agreed if he would also take her to her mother. She directed him to the cemetery where she placed the rose on a freshly dug grave. The man returned to the flower shop and canceled the order. Instead, he got in his car and drove 200 miles to his mother's home to personally deliver a bouquet of local flowers.

Without any uncertainty, I am convinced that success in life has nothing to do with what you gain in life or accomplish for yourself. It is what you do for others. George Bush said, "We all have something to give. So if you know how to read, find someone who can't. If you've got a hammer, find a nail. If you're not hungry, not lonely, not in trouble – seek out someone who is." The measure of life is not its duration, but its donation. Your life ought to be driven by a purpose and fueled daily by a healthy dose of passion and, most notably, by giving what we have and giving who we are. Making a difference is about purpose and passion, but it is also about pride. The pride in knowing that the more we share, the more that we have. Count your blessings, be a blessing and thank God daily for your blessings. Turn your dreams into actions and live your life to the fullest, minus the excuses. Take pride in everything you do and be ferociously persistent to become who you were intended to be so you can sow seeds that benefit others.

LIVE YOUR BOOK

The number one question I am always asked regarding my bestselling book, *Enjoy The Ride*™, is, "What was the biggest challenge in writing the book?" Living it! The old proverb, actions speak louder than words, is never more true than when you write a book and then are challenged to live it. How empty our words are when they are not sustained by our actions. As a parent, you take pride in being a mother or a father, so remember that children learn at a very young age that they are safer when they respond to what you do rather than what you say, if the two messages differ. When we say we will follow through on our share of the housework and then don't, our spouses quickly begin to question whether they can trust us. Many people will promise anything in the glow of the moment and do nothing in the heat of the day.

HOW EMPTY OUR WORDS ARE WHEN THEY ARE
NOT SUSTAINED BY OUR ACTIONS.

When we behave this way, the other person (or persons) is not the greatest loser. We are. When our actions do not fit our words, not only do we set off a negative chain reaction outside ourselves, we set off a negative chain reaction within ourselves. We learn not to trust ourselves, and we feed an unbalancing process within ourselves that leads to low self-esteem and uneasiness. We cannot be dishonest to others without being dishonest to ourselves. Look within yourself and have the pride to make your actions and your words congruent. When I cleaned up this part of my life and began to live my book, it was then, and only then, that I truly started to enjoy the ride.

GRAB HOLD OF LIFE

The famous author "Anonymous" was once quoted as saying, "The problem with life is that it is so daily." That's true. But if you are uncomfortable with that profound reality, consider the alternative. Thanks to medical science, people are living longer and longer. Unfortunately, many people have not learned to take advantage of the extra years. Quantity of life has not necessarily resulted in enhanced quality of life. For many people, life has become a process of daily existence and not much more. This daily responsibility called life beckons us to make the most of the possibilities and challenges, as well as the failures and setbacks.

Two young guys joined a construction crew commissioned to build a multi-story office building. At lunch they placed themselves on an iron girder high above the ground and opened their lunch boxes. "I can't believe it," blurted Joe, "peanut butter and jelly sandwiches. I don't like peanut butter and jelly." With that, he crumpled his sandwiches and hurled them to the ground. Lunch on the second day produced the same scenario as Joe became visibly upset with the sandwiches in his lunch. Once again, after a few bites he hurled the remaining sandwiches seventeen stories below. Joe's buddy dreaded lunch on the following day. Rather than enjoying a well-earned rest, he was stuck listening to his new co-worker complain day after day. He silently watched Joe sort through his lunch selection. Then it happened. "I've had it with peanut butter and jelly," screamed Joe. He angrily tossed the sandwiches in his hand and thrust them to the ground below. Unable to restrain himself any longer, Joe's buddy shouted, "If you don't like peanut butter and jelly sandwiches, then tell your wife not to make them anymore." "Wait a minute," Joe quickly exclaimed, "don't bring my wife into this. I make my own sandwiches."

We may chuckle at the absurdity of this situation, but it has a definite relevance to most of our lives. We all make our own sandwiches. Quality of life is determined by the ingredients we choose in filling the time between the two slices of bread – the beginning and end of our lives. It probably goes without saying that to enjoy the riches of life and make a difference in other people's lives, we need to make wise choices about what we fill it with.

CHASE THE RIGHT THING

According to a 1987 survey conducted by the American Council on Education, 75 percent of the 200,000 incoming freshman who were polled felt that being well-off financially is either an "essential" or a "very important" end to achieve. Seventy-one percent of the students said the primary reason they were in college was so they could attain high-paying jobs upon graduation.

Unfortunately, only 29 percent of these aspiring young people believed it was necessary to develop a meaningful philosophy of life. In Srully Blotnick's research reflected in *Getting Rich Your Own Way*, 1,500 people were divided into two groups and followed for 20 years. Group A made up 83 percent of the sample. These people were embarking on a career chosen for the reason of making money now in order to do what they wanted later. Group B, the other 17 percent, chose their career based on what they wanted to do now and would worry about the money later. The data revealed some startling discoveries. At the end of 20 years, 101 of the 1,500 had become millionaires. Of the millionaires, all but one – 100 out of 101 – were from Group B, the group that had chosen to pursue what they loved.

WEALTH IS ENJOYING WHAT WE ALREADY HAVE – NOT GETTING MORE OF WHAT WE THINK WILL MAKE US HAPPY.

According to this research, people who set out to make their million without serious consideration of their philosophy of life or what career would bring meaning and fulfillment are apt to be disappointed. Henry Ward Beecher had a point when he said, "Very few people acquire wealth in such a manner as to receive pleasure from it." Wealth is enjoying what we already have – not getting more of what we think will make us happy. Prior to becoming financially secure, I was really quite happy. I firmly believe I would have never acquired what I have today if I wasn't happy to begin with. A friend of mine, Jeff Dray, has, on more than one occasion, said, "You have reached the sweet spot in life." When I asked what he meant by the "sweet spot" his response was, "I know a lot of people who would love to do what you do, be where you are, and enjoy the things you enjoy." I believe that to be true. However, I also believe that my success is based on my philosophy of life. I believe there are risks and costs to achieving the so called *sweet spot* but that they are fewer than the long-range risks and costs of comfortable inaction.

"VERY FEW PEOPLE ACQUIRE WEALTH IN SUCH A
MANNER AS TO RECEIVE PLEASURE FROM IT."

My publisher asked me to speak at an Author Marketing Summit in 2010. At the summit, I addressed both seasoned authors and a large number of aspiring young authors who wanted to take their speaking careers to the next level. During my presentation, I offered to send anyone in the audience a copy of my best practices on how I wrote a bestselling book, and how I built a multi-million dollar speaking business from the ground up. One month after the summit, I had received only two requests for the information. So the moral to the "sweet spot" hypothesis is this – a lot of people have ideas, but there are few who decide to do something about them. When we do more than we are paid to do, eventually we will be paid more for what we do.

BE A GEYSER, NOT A MUD PUDDLE

Who would you rather be around? Someone who exudes vitality, enthusiasm and a zest for life or a pessimistic, downtrodden bore? When given the choice, the majority of people from all walks of life would rather befriend the optimistic, enthusiastic upbeat person.

Here's a case in point. General William Westmoreland was once visiting a platoon of paratroopers in Vietnam. During the conversation, the general asked this question: "How do you like jumping out of planes?" The first paratrooper responded, "I love it, sir." "How do you like jumping?" he asked the next. "It's a fantastic experience, sir!" exclaimed the soldier. "I couldn't imagine not doing it." "How do you like it?" he asked the third. "I'm scared to death, sir, and don't much like it," he honestly replied. "Then why do you do it?" the general queried.

"Because I love being around the guys who enjoy it." Do people enjoy being around you? Are you the type of person who attracts others because of your enthusiasm for even the undesirable tasks? If you want to be liked, show that you like life by your enthusiasm. Better to be a geyser than a mud puddle!

AFFLUENCE IS BEING RECURRENTLY HUMAN

Ever been around someone who is so impressed with themselves that they judge your behavior to be borderline emotionally disturbed? Their smirks are more evident than their phony smiles and braggadocios vernacular. They are not schizophrenic, but they do represent three people. The person they see themselves as, the person we see them as and the person they really are. True wealth and stature comes from depth, not height. Placing yourself above someone because of something you possess is the modern way of describing the act of fooling yourself. My inspiration for this paragraph is from a gentleman in seat 2A on a US Airways flight from Kansas City, Missouri to Charlotte, North Carolina. He had all but thrown a tantrum that his sport coat had not yet been attended to by the flight attendant. His initial phone conversation on his cell phone, to whom I assume was his wife, was beyond pretentiousness. His posturing was so outrageous, even the people in front of me looked back to see who this self-impressed person was. As for me, I was simply being entertained and inspired. He had just told the person on the other end of the phone that it had been so long since he had flown commercial that he forgot to take his shoes off going through security. The amusement of it all – I was behind him going through security and he didn't forget.

TRUE WEALTH AND STATURE COMES FROM DEPTH, NOT HEIGHT.

If he lived in the county where I reside, I am quite sure he would live in what I refer to as the "we're better than you neighborhood" – a gathering of people whose identity and stature is based on making sure you know where they live within 15 minutes of meeting them. I'll take the innocence, ignorance, and purity of friends and family who may not live in an expensive home, but have accepted that being human and who you really are is okay. For me, wealth lies within a person and is located somewhere between their heart and their soul. It is having the courage to identify yourself, know who you are and not let a person's social status change you. As for my seatmate next to me, I was just honored he lowered his standards and allowed us to be in his presence on this commercial flight. I guess his plane was up in the air just like his nose.

IN EVERY SITUATION FIND VALUE

My son, Josh, was always interested in any activity that involved a ball. My grandson, Karter, is exactly the same. Their favorite sport is solely dependent on the time of year. During Josh's stint playing t-ball, he became bored with hitting a baseball off a tee and wanted to play baseball like his older brother, Stephen. One Saturday morning, I observed him as he stood in the yard practicing his batting.

Throwing the ball into the air, Josh took a healthy swing with his new aluminum bat and missed. "Strike one," he screamed. Tossing the ball in the air once again, he swung and missed. "Strike two," his young voice declared. Repeating the action one more time, he, once again, failed to make contact. "Strike three, you're out!" Worried he wouldn't handle the disappointment, I walked over to give him some encouragement. He dropped his bat, wiped the sweat off his forehead and then proudly declared, "What a pitcher!"

Ever had a strikeout experience? There is a tendency to tear ourselves down, get hard on ourselves or give up when the final strike has been called. Take a lesson from Josh. Focus on the good. Even in the worst of circumstances, we still have value. Find it and make a difference!

PRIDE GOES BEFORE THE FALL

Whenever you discover true wealth, you will make a difference. Part of that process involves a modesty that allows you to impact people in a positive way. Anytime I get full of myself, I remember an incident when I finished speaking in Auckland, New Zealand and a couple from the audience approached me with a camera outside the auditorium where I was signing books. When I struck a pose for them, the man said, "No, no, we want you to take a picture of us." Dr. Joyce Brothers said, "An individual's self-concept is the core of his personality. It affects every aspect of human behavior – the ability to learn, the capacity to grow and change, the choice of friends, mates and careers." It is imperative that we bridle our egos and try to learn who we really are rather than telling ourselves who we should be. Until you make peace with who you are, you'll never be content with what you have.

Scott Epperson, a good friend of mine in the speaking industry, shared a story about the first time his wife, Melanie, attended one of his speaking engagements. He knew that his wife's approval would be the ultimate compliment as he endeavored to become a professional speaker. He feverishly memorized his key points, practiced his illustrations and rehearsed his stories. When he stepped on stage that night, he delivered what he told me was a flawless 45-minute speech. When he concluded, the crowd applauded his remarks. The pride swelled up inside him as numerous people shook his hand and thanked him for his speech. In the car on the way home, he turned to his wife and asked, "Sweetheart, how many great speakers do you think there are in the world today?" His wife, Mel, smiled, placed her hand on his hand and said, "One fewer than you think, Scott."

THE PURSUIT OF HAPPINESS

The Constitution only guarantees American people the right to pursue happiness. You have to catch it yourself. Happiness is not a possession we search for. Rather, it is a blessing present in everything we experience. It is imperative that we never let things we can't have, or don't have, or should have, spoil our enjoyment of the things we do have and can have. True wealth can be found by living in the moment and savoring it for what it is, not running ahead in anticipation of what is coming. Unhappiness comes from not knowing what we want and then killing ourselves to get it. Charles Kettering said, "Success is getting what you want, happiness wants what you get." I personally have been blessed 10 times over and, when I look back over my life, I realize that my life has never been absent of trials and misfortune, but I have been able to discover happiness in the midst of my adversity. By understanding that happiness is a conscious choice and not an automatic response, I have been able to enjoy times in my life that some may have found overwhelmingly depressing. Regardless of my position in life, I have, for the most part, maintained a disposition that chose to focus upon the good. So while the Constitution of the United States guarantees pursuit of happiness – we have to catch up with it ourselves.

LEARN TO LOOSEN UP

Laughter is a cheap medicine. It distracts your attention, changes attitudes and outlooks of life, causes relaxation and reduction of tension, while increasing the body's natural painkillers. In short, laughter relaxes our tensions and promotes feelings of well-being. Many people have become far too serious. Laughter lightens our moods and bonds us to others. By laughing with people, you will show them you are flexible and also reinforce that laughter is a good way to deal with stress, disappointments and change. Most importantly, it will bring happiness to everyone. Be sure to laugh at yourself.

Every year my wife and I host a Christmas party at our house and the people who attend are friends we been fortunate to meet along the way. They are there to lean on throughout the year and we are there for them in kind. They understand that we are busy and when we get together after a long absence, there is still a comfortable rapport. They attend the party with full knowledge that for one night, they will be given a gift, whether they accept it or not. That gift is the ability for each of them to learn to laugh at themselves. We play the newlywed game and, for people who have been married a long time, it is a riot to learn how much they don't know about their spouse. Some play the game to win, some play the game to survive the ride home, while others simply laugh at what they don't know about their spouse but should have. Of course, everything is always funnier as long as it is happening to someone else.

IN ORDER TO BE AN INSPIRATION TO SOMEONE
ELSE, YOU HAVE TO BE INSPIRED.

Loosening up allows you to stand outside of life's flow and view the whole landscape including the incongruities, the challenges outside our control and the unexpected. The difference we can make in another person's life begins with ourselves. The ability to enjoy what is funny and to laugh at ourselves can also enhance self-esteem and self-acceptance and help us cope with the difficulties of everyday life. In order to be an inspiration to someone else, you have to be inspired. Your cup must be filled first in order to impact someone else. Good humor is a tonic for the mind and body. It is the best antidote for anxiety and depression. It is a difference maker that makes you wealthy.

THINK DIFFERENTLY AND POSITIVELY

A blind boy sat on the steps of a building with a hat by his feet. He held up a sign that said "I am blind, please help." There were only a few coins in the hat. A man was walking by. He took a few coins from his pocket and dropped them into the hat. He then took the sign, turned it around and wrote some words. He put the sign back so that everyone who walked by would see the new words. Soon the hat began to fill up. A lot more people were giving money to the blind boy. That afternoon the man who had changed the sign came to see how things were. The boy recognized his footsteps and asked, "Were you the one who changed my sign this morning? What did you write?" The man said, "I only wrote the truth. I said what you said but in a different way." I wrote, "Today is a beautiful day but I cannot see it." Both signs told people that the boy was blind. But the first sign simply said the boy was blind. The second sign told people that they were so blessed that they were not blind. Should we be surprised that the second sign was more effective? Be thankful for what you have. Be creative. Be innovative. Think differently and positively. When life gives you 100 reasons to cry, show life that you have 1000 reasons to smile. Face your past without regret. Handle your present with confidence. Prepare for the future without fear. Keep the faith and drop the fear. The most beautiful thing is to see a person smiling. And even more beautiful is knowing that you are the reason behind the smile!!!

DO YOUR PART

One of my favorite stories is about the good and faithful man who fell upon financially hard times. Every time he turned around, it seemed another demand was placed upon him until finally, as the saying goes, he was "so poor he couldn't pay attention." One night in his distress, he dropped to his knees, lifted his eyes toward heaven and prayed, "Dear God, I am destitute. Please let me win the lottery soon!" The next week he was optimistic his condition would change. After three months, his faith began to waver and, by the end of the year, he became angry that he had not won a single dime.

"Are you there, God?" he pleaded. "I believed you would help me, yet an entire year has passed without you answering my prayers." Suddenly, a dark cloud appeared in the sky, lightning flashed and a voice boomed from the heavens "I hear you…I hear you. In fact, I've heard your every prayer, but give me a break. The least you could do is purchase a lottery ticket."

Those who say *what difference does it make* have decided to wait to be rescued from their undesirable circumstances and will undoubtedly wait a very long time. You can't hit a homerun unless you step up to the plate. You can't catch a fish unless you put a line in the water. You can't make a difference unless you actually do something. In the words of a famous shoe manufacturer "Just do it!"

GROW YOUR GRATITUDE

A growing body of research suggests that maintaining an attitude of gratitude can improve psychological, emotional and physical well being. At Thanksgiving dinner, many families join hands and take turns saying what they are thankful for. In our family, everything from pumpkin pie to iPhones, to family, friends and God are part of the discussion. Imagine what might come up if we shared our thankfulness at dinner every day and turned a holiday tradition into a way of life. I am constantly reminding myself of how blessed I am and thank God daily for those blessings. I am also quick to thank my wife for the many things she does daily so she knows how much I appreciate her thoughtfulness. Being grateful also helps overcome negativity and our tendency to dwell on problems, annoyances and injustices rather than upbeat events. Adopting a more upbeat mind set also helps facilitate gratitude. Instead of bonding with friends over gripes and annoyances, try sharing what you're grateful for. Focusing on blessings can help ward off depression and build resilience in times of stress, grief or disasters.

IMAGINE WHAT MIGHT COME UP IF WE
SHARED OUR THANKFULNESS AT DINNER EVERY
DAY AND TURNED A HOLIDAY TRADITION
INTO A WAY OF LIFE.

As I travel, waitresses, flight attendants and people I encounter in the service industry are all recipients of a "thank you" that comes from my heart. I usually shake their hands and let them know specifically what I am grateful for regarding their service. I am also quick to acknowledge my gratefulness for making it through some of the tough times and the strength I have been given to survive the hardships.

Interestingly enough, we tend to only focus on our thankfulness on that one Thanksgiving Thursday each year. It needs to become a habit that is a part of your daily routine.

Last, if you find you take too much for granted, try to imagine what life would be like without a major blessing, such as a spouse, a child or a job. Gratitude is good for you. Studies show grateful people are happier, healthier and better able to withstand hardship. Happier people make a difference.

SHARE THE WEALTH

Try spreading around some blessings and see what happens. Blessings come gently to our eyes and ears, tenderly caressing our being with love and compassion. They move through the cracks in our soul, healing them as they pass through. They give us images to fill voids caused by the wear and tear of the world. Blessings are a very easy and inexpensive way to pass around great treasures. They lighten us and fill us at the same time, while demanding nothing from us in return. Blessings can be given anytime, anyplace, openly or silently. It really doesn't matter, as both the blesser and the blessed are enriched. Below is an email I received after speaking at a convention in Indianapolis, Indiana which confirms that when you bless someone else you, too, receive the blessing.

I don't know if this message will get you Mr. Gilliland, but I just heard you speak at a convention on Tuesday, Nov. 16. I just wanted to say thank you for your words. I have heard people speak before but, no one has ever touched my heart. I just lost my sister on October 29, 2010 and your words just inspired me to want to be a better person and that it is never too late to achieve my goals, I never realized how much I take for granted. My sister left behind 4 children; a set of 18 year old twins, a 15 year old daughter and a 9 year old son. My brother-in-law is taking it hard, but with your words and your book, which I already read but have to purchase a copy of my own, I will share with him the right road to follow. I will make sure he takes a right. Thank you so much, I am not sure if you know just how much you can impact a person's life but you really helped me. I was sort of lost and didn't know which way to go, but now I know always go right and you will never go wrong. When I came home to my own 3 children and husband as well as my niece and nephew I just hugged them and told them how much I loved and appreciate them. I now remember that it is just the little things that count. Like dinner around the table, or taking the kids to the park so I can watch them play, or just sitting at home and asking everyone how was their day. I will take what I heard and read and use it as a guide to the life I want for me and family. Once again thank you Steve Gilliland for your kind words.   *Niccole Navarez-Martinez*

The deepest craving of human nature is the need to feel appreciated. You never know when a few words of encouragement can have an impact on a life. Numerous things have been compared to potato chips so let me add another. Compliments are like potato chips. One is never enough. You always look for more. Offering compliments based on a person's character or actions inspires them to perform in such a manner that invites additional praise. People tend to live up to the compliments they receive. When we know we have pleased someone, we have a tendency to want to do more to please.

True wealth is discovered when you begin to realize that your presence will either bring a person up or down. How are you bringing people up? What specific things do you do every day to show others their importance to you? Do you celebrate their success? People who make a difference set their self interest aside and rejoice in the happiness of others. Sharing the wealth is about encouraging other people to go for their dreams and cheer them on to make their ambitions become reality. Don't just give what you have, give who you are.

CHAPTER AFTERTHOUGHT

I wish you enough...

Recently I overheard a father and daughter in their last moments together at the airport. They had announced the departure. Standing near the security gate, they hugged and the father said, "I love you, and I wish you enough." The daughter replied, "Dad, our life together has been more than enough. Your love is all I ever needed. I wish you enough, too, Dad." They kissed and the daughter left. The father walked over to the window where I was seated. Standing there I could see he wanted and needed to cry. I tried not to intrude on his privacy, but he welcomed me in by asking, "Did you ever say goodbye to someone knowing it would be forever?" "Yes, I have," I replied. "Forgive me for asking, but why is this a forever goodbye?" "I am old, and she lives so far away. I have challenges ahead and the reality is – the next trip back will be for my funeral," he said. "When you were saying goodbye, I heard you say, 'I wish you enough.' "May I ask what that means?" He began to smile. "That's a wish that has been handed down from other generations. My parents used to say it to everyone..." He paused a moment and looked up as if trying to remember it in detail, and he smiled even more. "When we said I wish you enough, we wanted the other person to have a life filled with just enough good things to sustain them." Then turning toward me, he shared the following as if he were reciting it from memory.

"I wish you enough sun to keep your attitude bright no matter how

gray the day may appear.

I wish you enough rain to appreciate the sun even more.

I wish you enough happiness to keep your spirit alive and everlasting.

I wish you enough pain so that even the smallest of joys in life may appear bigger.

I wish you enough gain to satisfy your wanting.

I wish you enough loss to appreciate all that you possess...

I wish you enough hellos to get you through the final goodbye."

6

MAKE SOMEONE'S LIST

What you do for yourself

dies with you. What you do

for others is immortal.

MAKE SOMEONE'S LIST

O n October 30, 2009, I was the closing keynote speaker for the Association of Wisconsin School Administrators' conference in Wisconsin Dells, Wisconsin. The audience was made up of school superintendents, assistant superintendents, principals and assistant principals. Thirty minutes prior to being introduced as the guest speaker, I was approached by an elementary school principal who was wearing a t-shirt with their school name and logo on the front. He elatedly said, "I saw your name on the program and was thrilled to know I would meet you face to face. Earlier this year, I heard you speak at a leadership conference that I attended with my wife and we were blown away by your presentation. She suggested that I try and book you to speak at our school to open up the school year. However, when I called your office, I learned you were already booked on the day I wanted you." Overjoyed by his eagerness to book me and his comments regarding my presentation entitled *Making a Difference*, I was interested in knowing what he liked best about it. Without hesitation, he stated, "Make someone's list!" He then asked me a question. He said, "Do you know what Abraham Lincoln, me, you, my neighbor, Mother Teresa, Michael Jordan and the teachers at my school have in common? Every one of them is a person of influence. I challenged my teachers this year to remember how much influence they have when it comes to shaping a young person's life. I challenged each of them to impact a student in the coming school year, so much so, that if the students were asked to make a list of people who had influenced them the most in their lives, one of them would make someone's list."

THE POWER OF PERSUASION

When you look up the word "persuasion" in the dictionary you will see that it refers to influence, affiliation and advice. The people who are in your circle of association, universally known as your inner-circle, will be influenced by you. You don't have to be in a high-profile career to influence people. In fact, if your life in any way connects with other people, you are a person of persuasion. Your influence will either be positive or negative. People will either be drawn to you or deterred by you. You will either add value to a person or take it from them.

YOUR INFLUENCE WILL EITHER BE POSITIVE OR NEGATIVE.

As you raise your family, you are shaping a generation that will carry on your heritage, whether it is exceptional or ominous. Your influence will not be equal with all people. Having two sons, two stepsons and two daughters-in-law, I can attest to the fact that their interactions with other family members determine who they respond especially well to. It validates that your influence may not be as strong as that of someone else. Often when a divorce occurs, the children are subjected to numerous family contacts which can multiply the complexity of your influence and exactly how they respond. Small children are easily influenced by the gifts and adventure one parent may provide, while the other parent plays the role of the disciplinarian. Multiple family settings provide an array of values, rules and life perspectives. How your children discipline their children can often be divergent to your methodology. It doesn't make either of you wrong, only different. The good news is that you can still influence your grandchildren through the uniformity of your own life. Your intention should always be consistent and positive whenever you interact with people within your circle of influence and ultimately make that person's list.

LIVE YOUR MESSAGE

People will listen to what you say. However, they will watch what you do. If your actions don't match your message, then the inconsistency is a negative influence on the person's views of your perspective. If people perceive you to be positive and trustworthy, they will seek out your point of view. Unfortunately, unlike adults, children are inclined to follow what they see a parent or adult doing.

A LONE PERSON YOU INFLUENCE POSITIVELY TODAY HAS THE PROBABILITY TO INFLUENCE THOUSANDS OF PEOPLE TOMORROW.

As a professional speaker, I can provisionally influence a person. They assume I am credible and, if they observe me outside of the event, my actions will either confirm the message they heard or bust my credibility. I am grateful to have a wife who reminds me of my message and the duty I hold to live it. She reminds me at times when I may not be living up to a message that she knows I wholeheartedly believe in. She has never accused me of being duplicitous in what I speak about, only a little inconsistent in living it 100% of the time. As a matter of fact, one year when we were putting up the Christmas tree and I assured her it was secure moments before it fell over, she witnessed me get extremely upset over the entire situation. With a smile on her face, the tree laying horizontal on the floor and me ranting, she pronounced, "Enjoy the ride!"

As you interact with your family, your coworkers and everyone else you come in contact with every day, be aware of the fact your words and actions will touch them. The day-to-day interactions you have with people make an impact. One interaction with a person who is having a bad day can place a smile on your face and in your heart. A lone person you influence positively today has the probability to influence thousands of people tomorrow. You have an option to make a difference and add brilliant worth to another person's life.

LET YOUR EMOTIONS SET THE RIGHT EXAMPLE

As I left my career as an executive at a greeting card company, it wasn't from stress or burnout, I had simply lost my passion for what I was doing. Little did I know, at the time, that I was moving to something else that would help other people reach their potential. As a leader, I met a lot of good people in my eleven-year career that mentored me along the way. With that in mind, my new found purpose was to reach out to people who hadn't had the benefit of a great culture and invest time in helping them achieve their possibilities. I have always been drawn to people who have experienced similar journeys like mine who needed advice from someone who had made the mistakes and used them to grow and become stronger.

ONE MAN PRACTICING SPORTSMANSHIP IS FAR BETTER THAN 50 PERCENT PREACHING IT.

I'll always remember when Josh was a senior and got thrown out of a basketball game for fighting and being a central part of a fracas. After the game, I calmly let Josh know how I saw it. I explained to him that he allowed his emotions to help his opponent instead of his own team. I let him know that he had been blessed with talent. However, he would never excel in sports until he got his emotions under control and used them for good. He took note of my conversation and, by the time the spring of that year rolled around, he was playing baseball at a high level using his emotions for good. Today Josh is the head football coach at a high school where he is instructing young men that what you learn in life is the same thing you learn in football. You have losses, but you have to rebound from them. The key is how you bounce back from defeat and use your emotions to propel you in a positive direction.

One man practicing sportsmanship is far better than 50 percent preaching it. Josh came to realize that character is not built by lecture, but by a good example practiced day by day. I am convinced that Josh will make several people's lists by the time he hangs up the whistle. Most importantly, the people whose list will include Josh will have strength of character to be a lantern in the dark and make someone else's list.

THE LIST

What if everyone around you – family, friends, co-workers, neighbors, subordinates and every other person you have had the opportunity to influence were asked to make a list of the people who had influenced their lives the most? Would you make someone's list? If you made the list, why did you make it and if you didn't, would you be surprised? Would anyone who works around you or reports to you have you on their list? Have you been a person of influence and has it been positive? How many people's lists would you make? As you think about whose list you would be on, think about who would be on your list. Who has made a considerable difference in your life? Which people helped form the essence of who you are as a person?

MAKE YOUR LIST

Every person around you has an effect on you and your life. Some people will take more than they give and be an impediment. Others will add value to you and improve everything you do. These are people who will help take you to another level. So who makes the list? Who has added significance to your life? Who has played a major role in shaping your values, attitude and level of integrity? Who has taught you to be a great team player? Who trained you to be the person you are today? In the first chapter of this book, you made a list of people you admired. You listed the attributes and qualities you most admire in them. Now, I am asking you to think about who impacted your life the most. Who influenced you in such a way that you now find yourself responding to situations the way they did? Who was that mentor? I challenge you now, whether you're a parent, an educator, an executive, an aunt or uncle, to pass along the lessons of lasting value and make a difference. Make a list of people who have added value to your life, and ask yourself these questions. What did they give me? What values, characteristics and attributes are parts of me because of them? The people on this list made a noteworthy difference in your life because of how they influenced you and what they gave you. People on your list do not have to be well known. Their title, position and lack of infamy doesn't lessen their level of influence. The people who make your list will forever continue to influence others contingent on how you influence people.

PERSON OF INFLUENCE	THEIR INFLUENTIAL GIFT - WHAT THEY PASSED ON TO YOU

MY DIFFERENCE MAKERS

I consider myself the most fortunate guy in the world. I have had numerous people who taught me optimism, common sense and discipline. I had wonderful, strong women to teach me love and courage. I have returned the favor by being a mentor to others. Earlier in the book I challenged you to list the seven people you truly admire and the qualities you admire about them. Now, I am grateful to recognize several people who have made an enormous difference in my life.

DIANE GILLILAND – SUPPORTIVE

Marriages may start because of love, but they stay together because of dedication and support. There is a distinct correlation between family success and personal success. My wife, Diane, has helped me identify my purpose and expand my potential. She has built a strong family foundation and given my life deeper meaning. Lots of wonderful people have added value to me through the years, but no one quite like her. She completes my weaknesses and encourages my strengths.

Without her I may have been able to achieve some success, but with her my level of success has increased tenfold.

One person I am sure would make Diane's list is a person who influenced her life immeasurably and now has impacted me. It is apparent that, at an early age, she inherited her dad's love of people and I'm thankful she did. I never had the pleasure of meeting Bill Rohde, but many people who did said he was a wonderful and supportive person. His expansive personality and love of people allowed him to accept people and situations that others may have rejected. In Bill's common-sense world everyone made mistakes along the way, but he always accepted and supported them. Diane has always supported me even when I didn't exercise the best judgment and common sense.

THROUGH MY INADEQUACIES, SHE NOT ONLY
TAUGHT ME ABOUT THE POWER OF SECOND
CHANCES, BUT SHE HELPED ME EMBRACE
EVERYTHING THEY OFFERED.

She is a shining example of unconditional love and support. She has never once judged me for my past and, just as important, has always accepted me for who I am and what I believe. Regardless of my failures and deficiencies, she has loved me the same. Through my inadequacies, she not only taught me about the power of second chances, but she helped me embrace everything they offered. It was her fostering attitude that made me focus on my proficiencies and not my failures. I have accomplished so much more because of her spirit of approval rather than criticism. Even when I have let her down she has never withheld her love from me. She may acknowledge how my shortcoming upset her, but she continues to love me unconditionally. When you feel loved and supported, you can weather any predicament and truly enjoy all life has to offer. My success is because of a devoted and supportive wife who has, at no time ever left my side.

PAT WISE – GIVING

Regardless of our financial circumstances growing up, my mom always found a way to give. She always believed that giving is good for you and, not only can it make a positive difference in others, it can also bring you more meaning, fulfillment and happiness. She is, without question, the most giving person I have ever been around. She taught me to be selfless and filled with the strength of mind to give with no expectations in return. The church, family, friends, neighbors and numerous people less fortunate have been on the receiving end of her generosity.

When my stepson, Adam, was preparing to attend his first year at UNC-Charlotte, he was flustered over the cost of all the additional items necessary to attend college. He mentioned in a telephone call to my mom how outrageous a parking permit for the year was going to be. Four days later, a card arrived in the mail addressed to Adam and enclosed was a check for the total amount of the permit. Fixed income or not, she always finds a way to let generosity rule her spirit. She has always taken pleasure in giving gifts – something from her heart to your heart. Most of us take flowers or a bottle of wine when we are invited to dinner. My mom always keeps her eyes and ears open and picks out just the right little present to give, making it even more special.

SHE TAUGHT ME TO BE SELFLESS AND FILLED WITH THE STRENGTH OF MIND TO GIVE WITH NO EXPECTATIONS IN RETURN.

You don't have to "give until it hurts." You don't have to do anything big. Just being there for people with a servant's heart is more valuable than money and gifts. As a parent, my mom never saw her responsibilities just about being custodial and seeing to our health and well being. She gave so much more and was always giving by teaching, loving and conveying respect. Her generosity is what I remember the most growing up. She has impacted hundreds of people along the way and laid a foundation and example for me to follow.

JOHN SNYDER – LOYALTY

Some people reading this book will be surprised to see this name, and may perhaps be taken aback that I didn't shy away from including him as a person who made my list. However, it is easy to embrace an ingredient of my life that influenced me in so many positive ways. While divorcing his oldest daughter blemished his view of me, and irregular circumstances caused friction between our families, my ex-father-in-law taught me the meaning of trustworthiness, dependability and reliability. I have never met a person more loyal to his family and friends than John Snyder. His unconditional love was evidenced by his ability to accept your strengths and weaknesses intact. If he cared for you it wasn't because of what you could do for him, it was because he genuinely cared. He constantly paints a positive picture of his family and friends to others. Although he may hold them accountable privately, he is never critical of them to others. Moreover, he was always there to share in the joys and the sorrows. He never missed a football game, basketball game or baseball game his grandsons played. What's more, he never missed anything that involved his family. My remembrances include his devotion to so many people. He has never been too busy to help out or send a warm wish and a prayer their way.

HIS UNCONDITIONAL LOVE WAS EVIDENCED BY HIS ABILITY TO ACCEPT YOUR STRENGTHS AND WEAKNESSES INTACT.

When his daughter and I divorced, I can honestly say a father, a friend and a mentor vanished. He was a superb part of my journey and was the first male figure in my life that acknowledged he was proud of me. Although we went our separate ways, the instruction he provided and the influence he was made a great difference in my life. One of the final conversations we had included an uncommonly positive outlook regarding the direction I was heading. With the separation from his daughter pending and the uncertainty of what life was about to throw at me, he encouraged me to look in the mirror and do some soul searching. Even though he was troubled with who I had become and was saddened by the divorce, his stance was still that of loyalty. He was privately holding me accountable and, yet, cheering me on at the same time. He said, "I wish you nothing but the best and pray that you will bounce back and some day be very successful. When you do, I will be one of the first to say congratulations." For a number of years I did a lot of soul searching. I did rebound and today consider myself a person of positive influence. I am very devoted to my family and friends and have become the husband, father, grandfather and friend John expected me to be. John Snyder added a lot of value to my life and, while he may never have anticipated making my list, he did. His dedication to me for 22 years greatly enriched my life.

SHARON ALBERTS – PERSPECTIVE

As a die-hard Pittsburgh Steelers fan, I am always reminded of the first year Chuck Noll was their head coach. It was 1969 and the team had made "Mean" Joe Greene their first round draft pick. They opened Noll's first season as head coach by defeating the Detroit Lions at the old Pitt Stadium. Optimism hit an all-time high until they proceeded to lose their next 13 games. Isn't that incredible? A four-time Super Bowl winning coach started his career 1-13. What is even more astonishing is the Steelers only won four games the following season and had a losing record their second and third years under Coach Noll. If Art Rooney, the legendary owner of the Pittsburgh Steelers, had judged Chuck Noll's potential for success on his first three seasons, he would have fired him. But life isn't a snapshot, it's a moving picture. Nothing is better at helping you deal with failure than perspective. Just as Coach Noll's failure was not final, neither was mine.

PEOPLE WHO HAVE BEEN DOWN SO LONG WILL TRY AND RECRUIT YOU TO STAY DOWN WITH THEM. SINCE THEY ARE NO LONGER INTERESTED IN GETTING UP, THEIR GOAL IN LIFE IS TO PULL SOMEONE ELSE DOWN TO MAKE THEMSELVES FEEL BETTER.

Sharon A. Alberts taught me the true meaning of big picture thinking. As CEO of a non-profit company in Pittsburgh, Pennsylvania, she attended a leadership conference I spoke at in 1999. After attending the conference, she then hired me to speak to her leadership team. The irony of that speaking engagement would turn out to be that while I may have perhaps impacted her team with my message, it was her perspective that would impact me. "There will be other days," I remember her saying. From the very first time I was in her presence, Sharon taught me to see the big picture. For more than ten years now, I have had the pleasure of interacting with Sharon. She has shared in my successes and also my failures. She has motivated me to get back up when I have been knocked down. Her perspective has allowed me to *fail forward* and learn from my mistakes. Perhaps the most important viewpoint she has given me is to steer clear of people who are comfortable staying down. In fact, people who have been down so long will try and recruit you to stay down with them. Since they are no longer interested in getting up, their goal in life is to pull someone else down to make themselves feel better. Sharon is never down. She is either up or getting up! Her perspective on leading people is to use their failures to gauge their growth. She has an ardent approach to finding a person's strength and capitalizing on it. On more than one occasion, Sharon's perspective has stimulated me to discover other possibilities.

TODD CRISSMAN – FRIENDSHIP

A true friend is one who hears and understands when you share your deepest feelings. He supports you when you are struggling. He corrects you, gently with love, when you err and he forgives you when you fail. A true friend prods you to personal growth and stretches you to your full potential. Most amazing of all, he celebrates your successes as if they were his own. Who is Todd Crissman? Through thick and thin, Todd always came alongside me and experienced the difficult times with me and vice versa. I wasn't perfect and neither was he, but he has always brought out the best that was within me.

A TRUE FRIEND PRODS YOU TO PERSONAL GROWTH AND STRETCHES YOU TO YOUR FULL POTENTIAL.

I will always remember the first time Todd visited Diane and I in Mocksville, North Carolina. His eyes lit up and you could sense his pleasure as he toured our new house. His response was that of a true friend. "If anyone deserves this house, it is you. I am so happy for you and Diane. You have worked hard for not only this house, but everything you have achieved. I am proud of you. I always knew that even though you got beat down, you would get back up and be better than ever." Most importantly, he meant every word of it.

Todd has made a difference in my life that I am not sure I can even explain. When I was at the lowest point in my life and everyone else had turned their back on me, he never gave up on me. He always believed that there were no impossible problems and, that with enough time, thought and positive attitude, you can solve just about anything. He was absolutely correct! His friendship has never waned. He is the epitome of what a friend truly is. He always sees my faults, reflects them back to me and loves me through them. Todd doesn't always agree with me, yet he always welcomes my opinion even when our perspectives differ. He always offers me a perspective that no one else can. With so many people unable to let go of old resentments and grievances – Todd's friendship is not only special, but very unique. We have laughed together, cried together and shared so many special moments. It is always so relaxing to go out with my friend, Todd, because he already knows I am one-of-a-kind. No judging and no drama – just a friend who accepts me for who I am.

MARGARET SHANNON – AUTHENTICTY

"Just be yourself," Margaret would say as we were entrenched in yet another conversation that would ultimately improve me. Journey to greater authenticity begins when you identify the difference between what you believe and the truths you have inherited from others. Margaret Shannon, my former secretary, taught me to be more focused, centered, integrated, self-directed and purposeful. Your need for approval, acceptance, status, deference and even money diminishes as your authenticity increases. You become more dedicated to work that matters. Authenticity liberates and relaxes. It requires much less energy to maintain balance.

BECOMING THE LEADER SOMETIMES CREATES EMOTIONAL DISTANCE, BUT IT IS IMPERATIVE FOR YOU TO BE YOUR AUTHENTIC SELF.

Margaret also believed that part of our authentic self is driven by our ability to be straight forward. I will never forget what she told me the day I was promoted. She congratulated me and said, "Tomorrow two things will be true that are not true today. First, you will be the manager of this department. Second, you have heard the truth for the last time." She warned that becoming the leader sometimes creates emotional distance but it was imperative for me to be my authentic self. Authenticity is being you—the person you were created to be. This is not what most literature on leadership says, nor what the experts in corporate America teach. Instead, they develop lists of leadership characteristics one is supposed to emulate. They describe the styles of leaders and suggest that you adopt them. This is the opposite of authenticity. Margaret always said that all great leaders such as Abraham Lincoln, Martin Luther King, Jr., Winston Churchill, Anwar Sadat and Margaret Thatcher shared one thing in common—they were all authentic. She then advised me to be guided by my heart, passion and compassion, to be Steve Gilliland and no one else. Again, my voice was influenced and formed by a woman who had found her voice earlier in life and was willing to pass it on.

PAUL REED – COMPASSION

Compassion can move mountains and change lives. Growing up with divorced parents was not the norm in the 60's. As a matter of fact, I sometimes was angry that all of my other classmates had their mother and father living under the same roof, attending school functions together and providing an environment that I believed to be better than mine. My anger and frustration manifested itself in the form of defiance, dishonesty and lack of effort. Instead of turning his back on me, sending me to the principal's office or calling my mother, he chose to be compassionate and work with me before, during and after school. Even after I went to junior and senior high school, he would periodically check on me to see how I was doing. He never gave up on me and always displayed compassion for my situation.

IT IS YOUR LIFE EXPERIENCES THAT OPEN UP YOUR HEART TO HAVE COMPASSION FOR THE MOST DIFFICULT CHALLENGES THAT PEOPLE FACE ALONG THE JOURNEY.

He would never permit me to use my situation as an excuse. However, he understood that my circumstances were unique and, at the very least, he tried to understand. He taught me that you cannot live your life without compassion. It is your life experiences that open up your heart to have compassion for the most difficult challenges that people face along the journey. Far too many people wall themselves off from people who are experiencing the full range of life's challenges, hardships and difficulties. Unfortunately, the trends of our society shield us from the very experiences that open up our hearts. Mr. Reed taught me that every day we have opportunities to develop our hearts through getting to know the life stories of those with whom we work, taking on community service projects, having international students living in our homes, understanding the roots of discrimination and understanding that we all are not born into the same family circumstances.

Thanks to a sixth grade teacher, I learned how to develop compassion through intimate relationships with family, friends and coworkers and through having mentoring relationships. Mr. Reed's compassion was reverberating! He made a huge difference in my life and taught me how to care, share and be compassionate.

Although Mr. Paul Reed never traveled with me to speak, he has theoretically never missed a speaking engagement where my venue was education. His impact on my life was so great I always remind educators that they can change the world through one student. For the past 10 years, I have been blessed to speak at several school functions – mostly in August kicking off a school year. On August 23, 2010, I had the pleasure of addressing the faculty and staff of Central Community Unit School District 301 in Burlington, Illinois. The following is a letter I received which highlights my point to "make someone's list."

CENTRAL COMMUNITY UNIT SCHOOL DISTRICT 301
Dr. Todd Stirn, Superintendent
P.O. Box 396, 275 South Street, Burlington, Illinois 60109
(847) 464-6005 (847) 464-6021 Fax
www.burlington.k12.il.us

September 9, 2010
Mr. Steve Gilliland
P.O. Box 1600
Mocksville, NC 27028

Dear Steve,

I would like to take this opportunity to thank you for your inspiring and uplifting presentation on August 23, 2010. Your humor, life experiences and direct candor relevant to "making the list" has become a theme for the year for many of our administration and staff.

Your honesty concerning your experiences and the experiences of those individuals that you are surrounded with hit home to many staff members. I received more compliments regarding your presentation than I have ever received after any speaker we have had. Upon entering one of our elementary schools I heard the principal over the loud speaker remind staff to make their students' lists this year. As I watched teachers greet their students you could feel the positive energy of a new start. I believe they were ready to "enjoy the ride" of teaching while "making a difference" in the lives of students they touch, due in part to your message.

You touched each and every individual in the auditorium on August 23rd and your message continues to live in the hallways of the schools at Central District #301. Your message was clear, poignant and direct. Staff members walked out of the auditorium reenergized and with a clear focus of making a difference by taking time to get to know the student regardless of first impressions. Thank you for taking time to make a difference in the life of our staff at Central. You were truly inspiring!!

Sincerely,

Esther Martin
Director of Curriculum and Assessment
Central Community School District #301

Again, thank you, Mr. Reed. Your purpose-driven calling to make a difference as a teacher not only impacted my life, but continues to impact the lives of thousands. I'm not sure he ever realized how an elementary teacher in Pennsylvania in the late 60's would influence a child in an elementary school in Burlington, Illinois in the year 2010, but he did.

GIVE SOMETHING UP

I recently read about a father who, one evening after supper, settled into his easy chair with a stimulating book on investing. Barely into the first chapter, his vivacious and charming three-year-old entered the den. "Daddy," she said with that hard-to-resist tone of voice, "will you read to me?"` He looked at the title of his book, which guaranteed lifelong wealth, and then at his daughter's *Miss Piggle Wiggle*. "Hop up here, sweetheart. Let's find out what Miss Piggle Wiggle is up to." Giving means sacrificing our desires to meet the needs of others. This father realized that giving of himself would reap greater dividends than any investment strategy.

IT IS IMPOSSIBLE TO UNSELFISHLY GIVE OF
OURSELVES WITHOUT BEING BLESSED IN
RETURN.

It has been a blessing to see my son, Josh, with my grandson, Karter Paul. As a head high school football coach, he is constantly on the move and his schedule is very demanding. Add to the mix that he still loves to participate and watch sports and spend one-on-one time with his wife and extended family. Josh's time can be very limited. But when it comes to Karter, the Pittsburgh Steelers, Pittsburgh Penguins, most everything else takes second place. Playing hockey with Karter (in the living room which is not a favorite of mom) is only one of the activities I have seen Josh participate in with Karter when something else he enjoys is an option. He likes sports, but he loves Karter! It is impossible to unselfishly give of ourselves without being blessed in return. All that we send into the lives of others comes back into our own. Josh and my daughter-in-law, Kari, will reap the rewards in the future as it relates to Karter and any additional children they may have.

GIVE SOMETHING BACK

In his 1961 inaugural address, President John F. Kennedy said, "Ask not what your country can do for you, ask what you can do for your country." His words inspired a generation.

In order to make a difference in another person's life, first count the blessings in your life and constantly remind yourself of them. I receive a lot of emails and letters where people share their hearts, but none make the point of giving back better than a letter I received from a client and friend.

August 23, 2010

Dear Steve,

Tomorrow is my birthday, and I know that traditionally the honoree receives cards and gifts in celebration of the special day. But this year, I want to give on my birthday and here are the reasons why.

I have been very blessed in my life…physically strong, mentally able, and spiritually grounded. I have been tested along the way, but I am a child of hope. I look at each new day while standing firm on the promise that God forgives me and guides me if I choose to walk in His light. So I praise God for the blessings He has bestowed on me in this journey.

One of those blessings is a talent that I have always felt God gave to me to use for His glory and for educating and entertaining others. For over 30 years, I was a part of a church family where I shared my music in worship and in celebrations of life, such as the exchanging of vows and the home-going of saints. At the age of seven, I had the opportunity to play for a Tom Thumb Wedding in Austin for my grandmother's annual social event. Never before had a child sat at the bench to entertain on the stage in the downtown auditorium. I could go on about the opportunities that have been mine because of the gift of music. But for time and space, let me say, "Talents are blessings. "

I have been blessed by parents who accepted nothing less than my best and what was expected, was also given. They taught the values of being an interdependent member of a community at home, at church and in society. My parents were bold leaders who modeled integrity, loyalty and commitment to the organization who employed them. They utilized their creative inspiration to serve people in a more efficient way in both the educational and medical professions.

Years after the sudden mid-life death of my father, my mother was loved by my stepfather who took me as his own and said, "You are capable of doing anything you want to do. Take charge of your life." Some of you may already be laughing aloud and thinking…she has been taking charge for a long time, as the incident cited here will confirm.

Gammy [my grandmother] was preparing the meal and as usual, one of the helpers was taking drink orders and failed to inquire what I would like to drink. My response was quite direct, "Gammy is the boss of the tea, and I'm the boss of myself. So I'll have tea!" Reflecting on this event, I would say that this child was quite articulate and had a gift for analyzing situations with an acute ability to respond. I'm not sure my parents had the same opinion since I was about three years of age when I spoke those words. But whatever the opinion was at the time of this incident and perhaps others that followed, I am certain that my parents and stepfather played a big role in setting the mark for the expected level of achievement in our family.

I have been blessed to work in jobs that I really loved, not always easy, but jobs that enabled me to use my creative side to help others succeed. As a music educator, I was inspired as I observed students move from tentative to confident in sight-reading and expressive performance. As the principal of a school where the teachers gave selflessly for student success, I am deeply grateful. Since the school was named for an American war hero who was a respected leader committed to service to his camp, so were we committed to service to our community of learners.

I have been blessed by the love of my sister and brother. I'm not sure they thought having a little sister who got to practice the piano after dinner instead of washing dishes was a gift but they were as gracious as Mom and Dad expected them to be. Today, they are brilliant leaders in their professional life. They demonstrate the same qualities our parents instilled in me. They are blessed.

I am blessed by numerous friendships, some of which began in grade school and have continued through life. Others friends have crossed my path through work-related journeys, musical performances and unplanned meetings. To all, I thank you for your love and concern and continued faithfulness in our relationship.

Not last but intentionally saved for last are my very special blessings, Melissa, Michael and Natalie, my children. They are blessed. They too are physically strong, mentally able, spiritually sound and emotionally tender. They teach, model and give of their time to share the responsibil-

ity of soccer practices, piano lessons and more with their spouses. For their acceptance of parental responsibility, I am truly blessed.

My children are raising seven amazing grandchildren…Breyanna, Shane, Presleigh, Emily, Ben, Abby and Miles. They are intellectually inquisitive, athletically competitive and artistically creative. They have a zest for learning and laughter. They play hard. They accept responsibility in family life by helping with daily routines. These grandchildren are blessed. For all I have received, I am truly thankful.

Our family is blessed and although miles separate us, we are connected. We have a repertoire of accomplishments, most of which have been earned individually through the application of our natural talents and learned work ethics. We are blessed. So I invite you to share our blessings with a family in need.

I am working with a "Dream Team", a group of dedicated volunteers and residents at Marbridge in Austin, Texas. Marbridge is a home for those who are not as blessed as we are, if measured by physical, mental, social and emotional skill sets only. The residents have learning disabilities, physical handicapping conditions and often limited support from family members. The residents range in age from 22 and beyond. They are trained to develop workforce skills, athletic skills for competition in Special Olympics, creative performance skills for drama troupes and choral performances, independent skills for daily life and more. For many of the residents, this is home and family. This is the destination of their journey. So Marbridge makes the destination rich and fulfilling.

I became interested in Marbridge while working as a part of the "Dream Team" at the invitation of my coworker. The dream was to build a gym at Marbridge. The plan has changed because the programs offered at Marbridge are in need of a facility that supports experiential learning for its residents and the community. The revised dream is to build Victory Hall, an all-events center where athletic teams can practice and play competitively, a wellness center where all the residents can focus on fitness for life, a stage fitted for dramatic and musical presentations and a facility that community members can rent for private functions.

We believe this dream is going to become a reality. Our journey to raise over $2 million dollars has begun with the donation of the gym floor, the scoreboard and the wellness room. This is a start but we have not arrived at our destination. I am taking a step on this journey.

In your honor and in celebration of my birthday, I am making a donation to Marbridge. I ask you to consider joining me in this project. I am providing the link to the information about Victory Hall in this letter. The renderings of the building are on the page and some information about our dream. If you want to help make this dream a reality for the residents at Marbridge, I invite you to join me as we share our blessings with others.

Happy Birthday to me! Thank you for being a blessing in my life and may God continue to bless us all.

Love,

Cindy

http://www.marbridge.org/living/victory-hall.php

INDIFFERENCE IS THE OPPONENT TO MAKING A DIFFERENCE

As a Pittsburgh Steelers fan, I was delighted to witness them win their sixth Super Bowl title in Tampa, Florida. Who will ever forget Santonio Holmes and the catch he made with 35 seconds left in the game? But after the Super Bowl ended, a story surfaced about a missed opportunity to make a difference that was presented to current NFL players by Matt Birk, who at the time was center for the Minnesota Vikings.

Birk sent a letter to every active player, suggesting they chip in a share of their paycheck from the games of December 21 to help former players who were in bad shape physically and financially. Birk noted that some of these old guys don't have much of a pension and many are broken down from their days in pro football, when they helped build the sport into the land of milk and honey where it now costs $1,000 a ticket to attend the Super Bowl. "We are members of a brotherhood that lasts forever," Birk wrote. Any contribution would be appreciated. Large or small.

BE A PAIN IN EVERYONE'S NECK UNTIL SOMEONE DOES SOMETHING.

With 32 teams in the NFL all carrying active rosters of 53 players that meant 1,696 potential donors. Only 15 players responded. Not teams, but players. What's that tell you? Mike Ditka, one of the shakers and movers of an organization called Gridiron Greats, was saying, "Would you call it apathy?" Gridiron Greats is an organization of former players, many of them Hall of Famers, whose intentions are to help former players with financial and physical challenges. Like Ditka, Joe DeLamielleure, former player with the Buffalo Bills and current member of the NFL Hall of Fame, is also affiliated with this organization and said, "This group intends to be a pain in everyone's neck until someone does something."

The Super Bowl is over and everyone involved – Gridiron Greats and current players are still pointing fingers. But this is simple. The current players had a chance to make a difference. For one day they could have put aside all of the legal maneuvers and posturing between themselves and the league and they chose to think only of themselves. Somebody ought to remind these guys about Dwight Harrison. He was a cornerback for 10 years and now is a man in his 60's, struggling with the effects of too many concussions. He lives in a trailer, can't afford cable TV and can't get much help. Former Dallas Cowboys wide receiver, Michael Irvin, said it better than anyone regarding the situation. "While you're still on the field, you carry the weight to make a difference." Super Bowl XLIII is over, the bright lights have moved on and the current players are enjoying the offseason. Unfortunately, the pain and suffering the former players are experiencing has no offseason."

MY CORPORATE DIFFERENCE MAKERS

One of the questions I get asked most often is who do I regard as the preeminent examples of organizations that match my beliefs regarding purpose, passion and pride and truly make a difference.

Here are a few of my difference makers who enrich the lives of everyone they encounter. There are several others I could include. However, here are a few of my personal favorites.

IN-N-OUT BURGER

In fast-food corporate America, In-N-Out Burger stands apart. If you've ever heard me speak in person, listened to my CDs, watched a DVD or read any of my books, then you know why they make my list of businesses that make a difference. They are a lesson in a counterproductive approach to doing business that places quality, customers and employees over riches. They have cooked a billion burgers, hooked a zillion fans and provided a legendary business model. This is the epitome of a real American success story. It is not only a story of a unique and profitable business that exceeds all expectations, but it is a testament to old-fashioned values and reminiscent of a simpler time when people, loyalty and a freshly made, juicy hamburger meant something. Begun in a tiny shack in the shadow of World War II, this family-owned chain has become nothing less than a cultural institution that can lay claim to an insanely loyal following.

Why In-N-Out Burger makes Steve's list: From their first location in Baldwin Park, California in 1948 until today, their quality and consistency is an industry standard. They are a true culinary landmark and a West Coast staple. They are also a client of mine and I have had the privilege of speaking at their annual store managers' meeting.

STEVE'S FAVORITE LOCATION:
LAS VEGAS, NV (DEAN MARTIN DRIVE)
FOR MORE INFORMATION:
VISIT IN-N-OUT BURGER ONLINE AT
INNOUTBURGER.COM

MARRIOTT: THE SPIRIT TO SERVE

How does a $12-billion international giant that manages over 1,500 hotels under 10 different brand names with more than 3,400 food and facility contracts continue making a difference? The spirit to serve! From its humble beginning in 1927 as an A&W Root Beer franchise, Marriott has attributed its tremendous success to the passionate pursuit of that one clear vision and difference maker – the spirit to serve. Beginning with J. Willard Marriott, Sr.'s own personal commitment to continuous improvement, hard work and treating people well, Marriott's approach to business has evolved into a unique management philosophy based on fundamental core values and an unceasing quest to be the best. Their first location opened January, 1957 and only a few minutes after the ribbon was cut, the phone rang in the freshly painted lobby. The caller was inquiring about whether or not the Marriott's would like to purchase the new 48-room Disneyland Hotel in Anaheim, California. "Heavens, no!" Bill Marriott responded. "We probably won't be able to make this one work." Over 50 years later, they not only made it work, the Marriott family embodies that rare quality to which business leaders everywhere aspires – the ability to inspire in others a passion for great quality and service.

Why Marriott makes Steve's list: Like a strong family, a successful business is anchored in steadfast values and an unrelenting concern and respect for people. Marriott epitomizes the spirit to serve and even as big as they are, they remain consistent. You always know what to expect and, a high percentage of the time, they meet or exceed those expectations. If they fall short, they will rise up and make you want to come back again and again and again. They, too, are a client of mine who I have spoken for on more than one occasion.

STEVE'S FAVORITE LOCATION:
NEW YORK, NY (MARRIOTT MARQUIS)
FOR MORE INFORMATION:
VISIT MARRIOTT ONLINE AT MARRIOTT.COM

NORDSTROM

Ever since I can remember "customer service" has been the buzzword of American business, and Nordstrom has become the standard against which other companies measure themselves. Nordstrom is invariably cited by consultants, business school educators and authors of best-selling customer service books. Peter Glen, the customer service guru and author of *It's Not My Department*, says the Nordstrom shopping experience "can bring tears of joy to the eyes of customers." On his first trip to Seattle, Paul Smith, who was then North American director for Brooks Brothers' parent company, Marks and Spencer, told the *Seattle Times* in 1992 that when he first arrived in Seattle, he made a beeline for Nordstrom. After Nordstrom opened its first Midwestern store in suburban Chicago in 1991, commentator Paul Harvey told his national radio audience, "This store is teaching its eastern neighbors some manners." Harvey visited Nordstrom's Oak Brook Mall store, which happens to be the first Nordstrom I shopped in, three times in the first three days it was open. On the third day, he bought stock in the company. Nordstrom teaches practical lessons we all can apply in our professional and personal lives, including becoming "other centered" rather than "self centered."

Why Nordstrom makes Steve's list: Nordstrom's "wrote the book" on customer service and through four generations it has withstood the test of time. Their standards are what the rest of the industry shoots for. Morley Safer in a *60 Minutes* profile said, "It's not service like it used to be, but service like it never was." They have created a culture that gives employees freedom to think and act like entrepreneurs. The first time I ever visited a Nordstrom's, I was hooked.

STEVE'S FAVORITE LOCATION:
CHARLOTTE, NC (SOUTHPARK MALL)
FOR MORE INFORMATION:
VISIT NORDSTROM ONLINE AT
NORDSTROM.COM

SOUTHWEST AIRLINES

What started as a regional carrier serving Dallas, Houston and San Antonio became one of the airline industry's pioneering low-cost, no-frills airlines. Founded by Herb Kelleher and partner Rollin King in 1967, Southwest Airlines posted its 35th consecutive year of profitability in 2007. The airline has been known for campy antics. Flight attendants singing in-flight travel announcements to the tune of popular songs and pilots telling jokes over the intercom. Kelleher was even known to help load luggage, process tickets or mix drinks onboard. He says, "Happy employees make better employees. Your people come first, and, if you treat them right, they'll treat your customers right."

Why Southwest Airlines makes Steve's list: Ease of flying and the excellent level of service provided. I don't fly Southwest because of their low fares. I fly Southwest Airlines because they "get it!" Unless you are going on vacation, chances are you are only flying to get from point A to point B. Southwest makes it almost manageable to fly because of their unique approach.

STEVE'S FAVORITE DESTINATION:
HOME!
FOR MORE INFORMATION: VISIT SOUTHWEST
AIRLINES ONLINE AT SOUTHWEST.COM

WESTJET AIRLINES

WestJet was founded in 1996 by Clive Beddoe and a team of like-minded partners who believed that just because you pay less for your flight doesn't mean you should get less. Armed with that philosophy, three planes, five destinations and 220 friendly WestJetters, they began their journey. A journey that would take them to the 7,800 WestJetters flying 88 Boeing Next-Generation aircraft to 71 destinations in Canada, the U.S., the Caribbean and Mexico. My initial flight sold me on who I would fly when the opportunity (my speaking schedule) presented itself.

Why WestJet Airlines makes Steve's list: The first time I flew WestJet (Tampa to Toronto), I discovered their magical corporate culture. It's their planes that fly you places, but it's really their people who get you there. In fact, their entire corporate culture has been built around caring for you by providing a world-class guest experience. It's that commitment to caring that has seen them be awarded the title of Canada's Most Admired Corporate Culture by Waterstone Human Capital three years in a row. What they say in their ads is true – "Owners Care."

STEVE'S FAVORITE DESTINATION:
HOME!
FOR MORE INFORMATION:
VISIT WESTJET AIRLINES ONLINE AT
WESTJET.COM

CHICK-FIL-A

It all started in 1946 when Truett Cathy opened his first restaurant, Dwarf Grill, in Hapeville, Georgia. Credited with inventing the boneless breast of chicken sandwich, Mr. Cathy founded Chick-fil-A, Inc. in the early 1960's and pioneered the establishment of restaurants in shopping malls with the opening of the first Chick-fil-A restaurant at a mall in suburban Atlanta in 1967. With 42 consecutive years of positive sales growth, Chick-fil-A has set itself apart by ground-breaking innovations and delicious products. Armed with a keen business sense, a work ethic forged during the Depression and a personal and business philosophy based on biblical principles, Truett Cathy took a tiny Atlanta diner, originally called the Dwarf Grill, and transformed it into Chick-fil-A, the nation's second largest quick-service chicken restaurant chain with more than $3.2 billion in sales in 2009 and nearly 1,500 locations. His tremendous business success allowed Truett to pursue other passions, most notably his interest in the development of young people.

STEVE'S FAVORITE LOCATION:
WINSTON-SALEM, NC (HANES MALL)
FOR MORE INFORMATION:
VISIT CHICK-FIL-A ONLINE AT
CHICK-FIL-A.COM

7 Reminders for Building Children

by S. Truett Cathy,
Founder and Chairman of Chick-fil-A

1. Every child I know who overcame long odds and grew into a responsible adult can point to an adult who stepped into his or her life as a friend, mentor and guide.

2. Don't be too concerned that your children don't listen to you. But be very concerned that they see everything you do.

3. Be so consistent in your discipline that you're boring.

4. Stop arguing in front of your children.

5. You may think children have outgrown the desire to be rocked to sleep at night. They haven't.

6. Children will never believe in the covenant of marriage unless they see you living it with their own eyes.

7. How do you know if a child needs encouragement? If he or she is breathing.

Why Chick-fil-A makes Steve's list: From the beginning, the top priority for Truett and Chick-fil-A has never been to serve just chicken. Part of their corporate purpose is "to have a positive influence on all who come in contact with Chick-fil-A". They invest in scholarships for team members, character building programs for children, foster homes and other community services. I am a colossal believer in giving back so my admiration for S. Truett Cathy is expected.

RYAN'S RESTAURANT

Nestled deep in a wooded setting just minutes from downtown Winston-Salem, North Carolina and Wake Forest University, Ryan's has offered the Triad an escape from the ordinary since 1977. Ryan's chef creates a tantalizing selection of appetizers, and their juicy steaks and Maine lobster are the best I have ever eaten.

Why Ryan's Restaurant makes Steve's list: My family and friends have enjoyed the panoramic view of large oaks and a rolling stream from the many window-side tables and also savored the intimate atmosphere from a comfortable sofa, and in the winter, the warmth of a crackling fireplace. Besides the great food, their service is second to none. If you are ever in Winston-Salem, North Carolina, stop by and see why I have included my favorite restaurant in North America, Ryan's, in this book.

FOR MORE INFORMATION:
VISIT RYAN'S ONLINE AT
RYANSRESTAURANT.COM

HARRIS TEETER

Harris Teeter is a place where people say "hi" when you walk in, remember your favorite cut of steak and help you make sure your kids and your groceries all make it to your car safely. You get a fresh local food market with international flare, top-quality meats, seafood and produce, a commitment to excellence in customer service and satisfaction and, most of all, a company who has made the grocery store the heart of the community. Harris Teeter believes in giving back to the communities it serves. They focus their giving in five main areas: Eliminating hunger, educating children, promoting children's wellness, non-profit partnerships and disaster relief. They prefer to give directly to a non-profit organization with a specific project rather than fund-raising efforts such as golf tournaments, dinners or advertising. They are a leader in the grocery store industry.

Why Harris Teeter makes Steve's list: My wife drives past two competitor's grocery stores just to shop at Harris Teeter in Clemmons, NC. Her reasons are two-fold – great customer service and top-quality products at a fair price.

STEVE'S FAVORITE LOCATION:
TANGLEWOOD COMMONS, CLEMMONS, NC
FOR MORE INFORMATION:
VISIT HARRIS TEETER ONLINE AT
HARRISTEETER.COM

TRANSITIONAL SERVICES, INC.

They are an innovative human services organization transitioning people with mental disabilities (psychiatric and intellectual) into the community. Since its incorporation in 1969, TSI has offered eligible adults the housing and support services necessary to live successfully in the community. TSI serves more than 400 individuals each year throughout Allegheny County in Western Pennsylvania. TSI embraces a person-centered approach to service delivery. Using the Psychiatric Rehabilitation Approach and Everyday Lives Philosophy, staff assists individuals with the identification of personal strengths, skill building and empowerment. The goal of these efforts is to enable the individual to achieve role recovery. That means defining and resuming life on their terms. The development of natural supports is also an important focus. With more than 130 dedicated and caring employees, they are committed to supporting individuals with disabilities.

Why Transitional Services makes Steve's list: TSI believes that its employees are its greatest asset.

FOR MORE INFORMATION:
VISIT TRANSITIONAL SERVICES ONLINE AT
TRANSITIONALSERVICES.ORG.

CHAPTER AFTERTHOUGHT

Whatever issue or cause you're most passionate about, you can find a way to make a difference and continue to change the world.

DO YOU...
VOLUNTEER AT A NURSING HOME AND CREATE MEMORIES TO TREASURE?

According to the National Center for Health Statistics, more than 50 percent of nursing home residents have no close relatives, and 46 percent have no living children.

DO YOU ...
VOLUNTEER AT FOOD BANKS OR HOMELESS SHELTERS?

At the Food and Nutrition Service, you can develop and improve programs that provide meals to children and adults in day care centers, nursing homes, Head Start centers and family day care homes.

DO YOU ...
CLEAN UP PARKS AND STREAMS OR ORGANIZE RECYCLING PROGRAMS?

At the National Park Service, you can protect forests, manage wildlife and lakeshores and present educational programs to children and families about the conservation of cultural and natural resources.

DO YOU ...
TRAVEL TO LESS–DEVELOPED COUNTRIES TO TEACH OR VOLUNTEER?

At the Foreign Agricultural Service, you can administer grants for programs that combat hunger and malnutrition, promote sustainable development and encourage the growth of democratic participation in developing countries.

DO YOU...
MAKE YOUR SPOUSE'S DAY OR CHILD'S DAY?

At home, you can listen, communicate and participate. You can provide a little thought and a little kindness, which is worth more than money. You can remind yourself of what makes them special.

AN INTERVIEW WITH STEVE GILLILAND

Up Close and Personal

ADVANTAGE: IT HAS BEEN FIVE YEARS SINCE YOU WROTE *ENJOY THE RIDE*. WHAT HAS BEEN THE MOST PLEASANT OUTCOME FROM WRITING THE BOOK AND THE BIGGEST SURPRISE?

Steve Gilliland: The most pleasant outcome has been the number of people who have contacted me and let me know how much the book impacted them. The biggest surprise I encountered while writing my first book was re-reading what I wrote the day before. Several times I thought I was in "the zone" only to recognize I was in the twilight zone.

ADVANTAGE: YOU ARE A BIG BELIEVER IN CREATING EMOTIONAL VALUE WHEN YOU SPEAK, CAN YOU ELABORATE ON THAT?

Steve Gilliland: Audiences want a relationship with you and your message. If there is no emotional involvement, there is no connection to your message. While people are motivated by several factors, it's the emotional component that ultimately influences people. To create emotional value you have to personalize your message.

ADVANTAGE: WHY IS DEVELOPING A VISION SO IMPORTANT TO MAKING A DIFFERENCE?

Steve Gilliland: As a professional speaker and author, I must identify a need that isn't being met by someone else and how my message from the platform, or the pages in a book, can satisfy that need. All of that comes from a vision. To be successful, it is imperative that I understand the unique reason for my message, and then satisfy the unmet need of everyone who hears me speak or reads my books. Without vision, I have no direction. Without direction, I have no purpose.

ADVANTAGE: AT A RECENT ECONOMIC FORUM IN CHINA, WORLD LEADERS ANNOUNCED THAT OUR BIGGEST CRISIS IS NOT FINANCIAL, BUT RATHER A LACK OF TRUST AND CONFIDENCE. HOW DO YOU BUILD TRUST AND LOYALTY?

Steve Gilliland: Trust doesn't start with the economy, government or any other faction. It starts with individuals being trusted. Those who are most trusted enjoy the greatest impact and usually the bigger bottom-line. If you want to impact people and make a difference, your number one priority should be building trust.

ADVANTAGE: AS A SUCCESSFUL AUTHOR, SPEAKER AND BUSINESSMAN, DO YOU CONSIDER YOURSELF A WORKA-HOLIC?

Steve Gilliland: Great question and one that I am sure my family will want to read the answer to. I will say no, but explain why. I believe workaholics participate in destructive behaviors that impact themselves and others. They run themselves ragged and alienate people who love them the most. A workaholic does everything for the power and money and then one day they wake up and start to question whether all the stress was worth it. I am not stressed about my work and I am not driven by power or money. I am driven by a purpose to impact people. I have never been driven by money!

ADVANTAGE: I NOTICED YOU HAVE A SPEECH ENTITLED LEADING WITH HEART. DO YOU BELIEVE LEADERS CAN BE TENDER?

Steve Gilliland: Tenderness is greater proof of caring than the most passionate of vows. We have developed a mistaken belief that tenderness can make us vulnerable and, as a leader, most people are afraid to be vulnerable. Nothing could be farther from the truth of reality. Tenderness requires greater strength, not less. I challenge every leader to take a risk in the direction of tenderness and see what happens.

ADVANTAGE: WHEN YOU SPEAK, YOU USE A LOT OF HUMOR. HOW DO YOU THINK THAT IMPACTS AN AUDIENCE?

Steve Gilliland: I realize humor isn't for everyone. It's only for people who want to have fun, enjoy life and feel alive. Seriously, almost every aspect of our lives has the potential for having some humor in it. Every serious issue has a funny side.

ADVANTAGE: WHAT IS ONE OF THE BIGGEST LESSONS YOU HAVE LEARNED IN LIFE?

Steve Gilliland: WOW! I have learned so many, due to a plethora of mistakes, so narrowing it down is a test. However, I would have to say the biggest lesson I learned was looking at something I was trying to control and stepping back and seeing what a ridiculous solution trying to control it was. When I finally determined to let go and see what would happen, the results were astonishing. I have learned to participate more and control less.

ADVANTAGE: YOU HAVE DESCRIBED YOUR MOM AS BEING A PRAYER WARRIOR. WHAT MAKES HER SO UNIQUE?

Steve Gilliland: She doesn't spend a lot of time praying for things, she prays for people, including those people who have wronged her. She isn't perfect and we have our differences. However, when she says she is going to pray for you, unlike some people who say it to be heard and impress someone, she actually does!

ADVANTAGE: A LOT OF MOTIVATIONAL SPEAKERS SPEAK ABOUT THE IMPORTANCE OF SELF-TALK. WHERE DO YOU STAND ON THAT SUBJECT?

Steve Gilliland: I firmly believe your actions and your image of yourself are inextricably linked. They cannot be separated. You are what you do. You do what you are. As much as you might try to mask who you are or portray a certain image to the world, what you are will eventually reveal itself through what you do – the words you speak, the things you do, the activities in which you engage, the choices you make, the decisions you reach, the people with whom you align yourself and the work you produce. Equally true, the words that you hear, the experiences you take into your life, the consequences of your choices, the work you pursue, the relationships you have, all create who you are. The primary function of self-talk is to reinforce a positive image. Just as we program a computer, we have to program our personal computer. Now the short answer: Self-talk is very important!

ADVANTAGE: IF YOU WERE GIVING ADVICE ON PERSONAL DEVELOPMENT TO ENRICH A PERSON'S LIFE, WHAT WOULD BE YOUR BEST TIP?

Steve Gilliland: Read and listen. Engage in a personal development reading program that includes biographies of successful people. Peruse the self-improvement aisle of your favorite bookstore. The more you read, the more you will see what successful people have in common and how they more than likely had beginnings similar to yours.

ADVANTAGE: EARLIER IN THE BOOK YOU TALKED ABOUT E-STRACTIONS AND ALL THE TECHNOLOGY THAT HAS SEEMINGLY INTERFERED WITH OUR ABILITY TO BALANCE OUR LIVES AND REDEFINE OUR FOCUS. IS IT POSSIBLE TO MANAGE OUR TIME?

Steve Gilliland: No! You cannot manage your time and it isn't about balancing your time. It is about managing the activties that consume our time and balancing our energy and our attention.

ADVANTAGE: YOU ALSO TALK ABOUT ACCEPTING RESPONSIBILITY FOR YOUR ACTIONS, BUT DOESN'T FATE PLAY A ROLE IN WHAT HAPPENS TO EACH OF US?

Steve Gilliland: The first step is accepting your role in any situation. You can't blame other people. You can't blame fate. You can't fall victim to the notion that your circumstances were totally due to forces beyond your control, regardless of what they might be. All this does is reinforce the theory that you have no control over your life and what happens to it. I believe you create your own luck. You create what happens to you, based on your

*decisions. You create your future, both by your actions and your
inactions.*

ADVANTAGE: WE ADMIRE THAT YOU ARE OUR BEST-
SELLING AUTHOR AND THAT YOU HAVE BUILT A MULTI-
MILLION DOLLAR COMPANY, BUT WHEN YOU LOOK BACK
AT EVERYTHING THAT HAPPENED IN YOUR LIFE, CAN
YOU HONESTLY SAY YOU THOUGHT YOU WOULD END UP
WHERE YOU ARE TODAY?

*Steve Gilliland: It sounds like a trick question. To end up where
I am today took both perseverance and an iron will. Maybe more
important, it took an unyielding belief in my own vision. When
people fail, it's often not the inherent goal that was wrong or
misguided, it was simply that the means to that goal were inap-
propriate. You must be able to separate your vision from the path
to that vision. Sometimes it's just the route you take that has to
be altered. If you believe in something, regardless of the failures
on the road to that dream, you have to stick to what you believe.
And it never hurts to have a spouse who believes in you as much
as you believe in yourself.*

DIFFERENCE MAKER™

At Steve Gilliland, Inc. we are committed to guiding and encouraging people to be a Difference Maker™. By choosing to be a Difference Maker™, you are signifying your desire to grow and reach your potential and sow seeds that benefit others. We are excited to introduce our Difference Maker™ program and help you accelerate your learning experience.

AS A DIFFERENCE MAKER™
YOU WILL RECEIVE:

- What Steve Gilliland is reading. Steve will recommend a must-read book every quarter that he has recently read. He will send you his summary of the book, his personal notes and why he liked the book. Impact Store®, a division of Steve Gilliland, Inc., will also make the book available for purchase at http://www.impactstore.com or by calling toll free 1-877-499-8901.

- The Difference Maker Magazine. A full color periodical every quarter, complete with articles and interviews featuring well-known people who have made a difference. It also includes tips, quips and quotes from North America's most popular speaker, Steve Gilliland. In addition, the magazine will feature special articles on performance essentials and leadership essentials. This magazine is intended for today's professionals.

- Difference Maker™ Webinar. You will have access to four webinars in a calendar year featuring Steve Gilliland live. If you've heard him speak live, then you'll realize what a huge offering this is. He makes a difference!

TO BECOME A DIFFERENCE MAKER™, LOG ON TO: WWW.PURPOSEPASSIONPRIDE.COM AND CLICK ON THE **REGISTER** LINK IN THE UPPER LEFT HAND CORNER.

OUR MAIN PURPOSE IN LAUNCHING THIS PROGRAM IS TO HELP YOU MAXIMIZE YOUR POTENTIAL. NOW THAT YOU HAVE READ STEVE'S BOOK, MAKING A DIFFERENCE, SET ASIDE TIME EVERY QUARTER AND ALLOW HIM TO HELP YOU GROW PERSONALLY AND PROFESSIONALLY.

HOW LONG DID IT TAKE YOU TO WRITE THIS BOOK?

I am often asked, "How long did it take you to write this book?" To correctly answer the question with regard to this book, I pre-determined that I would give a glimpse of the first day and the final day. I wanted to pay homage to where I was on the day I set in motion writing the book and where I was the day I completed writing the book. So here is a peek with reference to the first and final day of typing the pages that make up this book, *Making a Difference*.

THE FIRST DAY

It is November 6, 2009, at 9:05 PM and I am on US Airways Flight Number 704 on my way to Frankfurt, Germany where I will connect to Lufthansa Flight Number 5716 which will take me to my final destination of Venice, Italy. I am scheduled to speak at 9:00 AM the next day for the Canadian-based company, Custom House, at The Westin Europa & Regina. I am very excited about speaking in Venice, but even more excited that I have transported with me four hanging file folders approximately three inches thick. The contents of these folders are a collection of articles, written notes and ideas that I have accumulated over a twenty-year period of time with the intent of someday writing a book about purpose, passion and pride. The title of the book was not yet determined until I came across a quote by Martin Luther King, Jr.

> "EVERYBODY CAN MAKE A DIFFERENCE…
> YOU DON'T HAVE TO MAKE YOUR SUBJECT AND
> VERB AGREE TO MAKE A DIFFERENCE.
> YOU ONLY NEED A HEART FULL OF GRACE,
> A SOUL GENERATED BY LOVE."

It is at that moment I am 100% positive the title will be, *Making a Difference*. Within minutes I am reading a quote from Hugh Black that says, "The very first condition of lasting happiness is that a life should be full of purpose, aiming at something outside of self. I pull out my computer, plug it into the seat outlet and inform the flight attendant that I probably will not be sleeping tonight and may need an extra cup of coffee or 10. She smiles and jokingly informs me that she probably won't sleep either and will check in on me periodically. My computer is ready to go and I begin by appropriately dedicating the book to my loving wife, Diane.

THE FINAL DAY

I am in Stowe, Vermont, speaking at the annual Vermont SHRM State Conference where the attendees have gathered at the Stoweflake Mountain Resort & Spa for three days to enhance their professional development. I am scheduled to close the conference on Thursday, October 28, 2010 at 1:30 PM. My closing keynote is entitled, Making a Difference, A Matter of Purpose, Passion & Pride™. I am excited to inform the audience that I have finished my new book and have included their conference and Stowe, Vermont, as the location where

I completed writing the book. So, as they say in show business, it's a wrap! The only thing remaining is to reread the book myself and then let the person I dedicated the book to be the first to read the manuscript. And speaking of my wife, Diane...below is an email I just received from her congratulating me on finishing the book.

Congratulations! You are the cheese to my macaroni, you are the horizon to my sky, you are the bacon to my eggs, you are the laces to my sneakers, you are the jelly to my peanut butter, you are the smile to my face, you are the gravy to my mashed potatoes, you are the bubbles to my bath, you are the milk to my cookie, you are the ink to my pen, you are the ketchup to my french fries, you are the water to my ocean and you are the icing on my cupcake. You are the person who has made the biggest difference in my life. Thank You!

Your Proud Wife

AFTERWORD

Tom Peters stated, "Instant, mindless cutting of marketing, salaries and bonuses in the face of a downturn is often counterproductive – or rather, downright stupid. Tough times are golden opportunities to get the advantage on those who respond to bad news by panicky across-the-board slashing." With everyone's attention centered on the economy, naysayer's forecasting the worst and the media continuing to fan the flames just a bit, it has become alarmingly obvious to me that people are overreacting and sending the wrong message to themselves and others. As I wrote this book, I read a newsletter from a colleague in the speaking industry who outlined what it would take to survive these tough times. I couldn't help but wonder if his advice would make a difference or make the state of affairs seem even worse. In the same article, he touched on the fight that loomed within our government regarding the bailout and whether or not it would help. Again, my opinion is that it was a negative outlook on a controversial subject that made me say, "How is this helping me endure these challenging times?" Just last week, I was on a conference call with a potential client who said the committee who selects the keynote speaker for their conference was leaning toward hiring an economist. No disrespect toward the committee or the economist, but is listening to someone tell people the economy will get worse before it gets better, that this is a short-term cyclical challenge and they will be asked to tighten their belt and do more with less going to really make that much of a difference?

NEVER LET YOUR SURROUNDINGS OR CIRCUM-STANCES CONTROL YOUR ATTITUDE.

We can't control the economy, influence a bailout or set policies that unravel the fiscal challenges we are facing. But we can make a difference. Prior to boarding a recent flight to Chicago, I observed a gate agent for American Airlines handling a disgruntled passenger. She was polite, focused and extremely calm. After she resolved the issue, I approached her and offered a compliment. She smiled and said, "It only takes a kind word to repel a bad attitude and make the situation appear endurable." She went on to say, "Just because the economy is tough right now, it's no excuse for being negative. I believe that if you let your surroundings control your attitude, it says something about who you really are." This woman had just confirmed for me that in spite of what seemed to be an insurmountable situation, she was able to change a person's outlook by simply staying positive. She made a difference! There is no handbook that tells you how to make a difference and navigate these challenging times. However, there are two things that you can do daily that will have a wonderful impact on your outlook. Count your blessings and remind yourself of what is really important. Regardless of the current situation, there is always something to be thankful for. I am appreciative for the birth of my first grandson (Karter Paul). I'm indebted to the numerous clients who have hired me to speak over the last 10 years. I am even thankful for the great cup of coffee I just consumed at Dunkin' Donuts after speaking. As for the important things in life, they are usually free. Your spouse, your children and your friends don't change when the economy is depressing. You need to amend the way you define success and realize that it isn't something you acquire or achieve. Success is the journey you take your whole life. It is how content and happy you are no matter what the circumstance.

I firmly believe it is a time to refocus, reignite your passion and climb to another level. It is time to accept the reality that everyone can make a difference despite the challenges we face. Making a difference doesn't require a college degree. You don't even have to make your subject and verb agree. It doesn't require money, fancy clothes or even a nice car. It isn't held in reserve for a select few and only worth something if given by a particular person. It has no age, race or gender requirements. It is about a smile, a kind word, a listening ear, an honest compliment or the smallest act of caring, all of which have the potential to turn a life or situation around. You only need a heart filled with love and a soul that cares. It has been said that giving makes you wealthy. Count your blessings, reassess your priorities and stop listening to the cynics. God-given ability and numerous circumstances may be out of your control, but the ability to make a difference isn't.

STEVE GILLILAND IS ONE OF NORTH AMERICA'S PREMIER KEYNOTE SPEAKERS. THE LIST OF 800 CLIENTS WHO HAVE HEARD HIS MESSAGE IN THE LAST 12 YEARS IS A WHO'S WHO DIRECTORY OF FORTUNE 500 COMPANIES, NATIONAL AND STATE ASSOCIATIONS AND COMPANIES BOTH LARGE AND SMALL. HE IS THE AUTHOR OF SEVERAL BOOKS INCLUDING HIS BESTSELLER, *ENJOY THE RIDE*™, AND HAS APPEARED ON RADIO AND TELEVISION ACROSS THE NATION. FOR MORE INFORMATION, PLEASE VISIT HIS WEBSITE AT WWW.STEVEGILLILAND.COM.

CHARITIES
TOP 10 LISTS
(Based on statistics compiled when the book was written)

LARGEST INDIVIDUAL DONORS TO CHARITIES

1. Stanley and Fiona Druckenmiller (Finance)
2. John M. Templeton (Finance)
3. Bill and Melinda Gates (Technology)
4. Michael Bloomberg (Media/Entertainment)
5. Louise Dieterle Nippert (Family Wealth/Investments)
6. George Soros (Finance)
7. Eli and Edythe Broad (Finance/Real Estate)
8. J. Ronald and Frances Terwilliger (Real Estate)
9. William Clements, Jr. (Oil)
10. Pierre and Pam Omidyar (Technology)

LARGEST RECIPIENTS OF PRIVATE DONATIONS

1. United Way Worldwide
2. Salvation Army
3. Fidelity Charitable Gift Fund
4. Food for the Poor
5. Feed the Children
6. Brother's Brother Foundation
7. AmeriCares Foundation
8. American Cancer Society
9. YMCA
10. Schwab Charitable Fund

OUR CHARITIES

Connecting People Who Care With
Causes They Care About

A FINAL THOUGHT

You've heard it asked, "What would you do if you knew you only had six months to live?" Who says you have six months? What are you doing now to make a difference?

Martin Luther King, Jr. exclaimed, "Even if I knew the world would end tomorrow, I would plant a tree today." Consider Saint Augustine. While weeding his garden one morning, he was asked, "What would you do if you knew you were going to die before the sun went down?" Without a moment's hesitation Saint Augustine responded, "I would continue hoeing my garden." These two men who were caught up in their purpose and time, or lack of it, would not alter their life's course. I have always asked the question in an interview, "Would winning the lottery change your daily routine?" If it would, then is your daily routine driven by a purpose?

In contrast, a person who possesses the best life has to offer can still be empty and directionless inside. Where you live, the money you possess, the money you stand to inherit, your marriage, the car you drive and the friends you appear to have are outward signs of success and not necessarily indicators of inner fulfillment. The amount we earn or the success we achieve produces emptiness unless it is in line with a purpose beyond ourselves. Like many, I searched for my purpose in life for quite some time. Happily, I have found that purpose in marrying my beautiful wife, Diane, guiding four beautiful children, Stephen, Josh, Adam and Alex, and sharing my heart in another book, *Making a Difference.*

{ *"The greatest use of life is to spend it for something that outlasts it."*

William James }

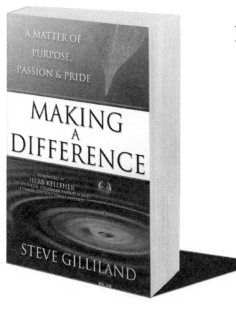

How can you use this book?

MOTIVATE

EDUCATE

THANK

INSPIRE

PROMOTE

CONNECT

Why have a custom version of *Making A Difference*?

- Build personal bonds with customers, prospects, employees, donors and key constituencies
- Develop a long-lasting reminder of your event, milestone or celebration
- Provide a keepsake that inspires change in behavior and change in lives
- Deliver the ultimate "thank you" gift that remains on coffee tables and bookshelves
- Generate the "wow" factor

Books are thoughtful gifts that provide a genuine sentiment that other promotional items cannot express. They promote employee discussions and interaction, reinforce an event's meaning or location and they make a lasting impression. Use your book to say "Thank You" and show people that you care.

Making A Difference is available in bulk quantities and in customized versions at special discounts for corporate, institutional and educational purposes. To learn more please contact our Special Sales team at:

1.866.775.1696 • sales@advantageww.com • www.AdvantageSpecialSales.com